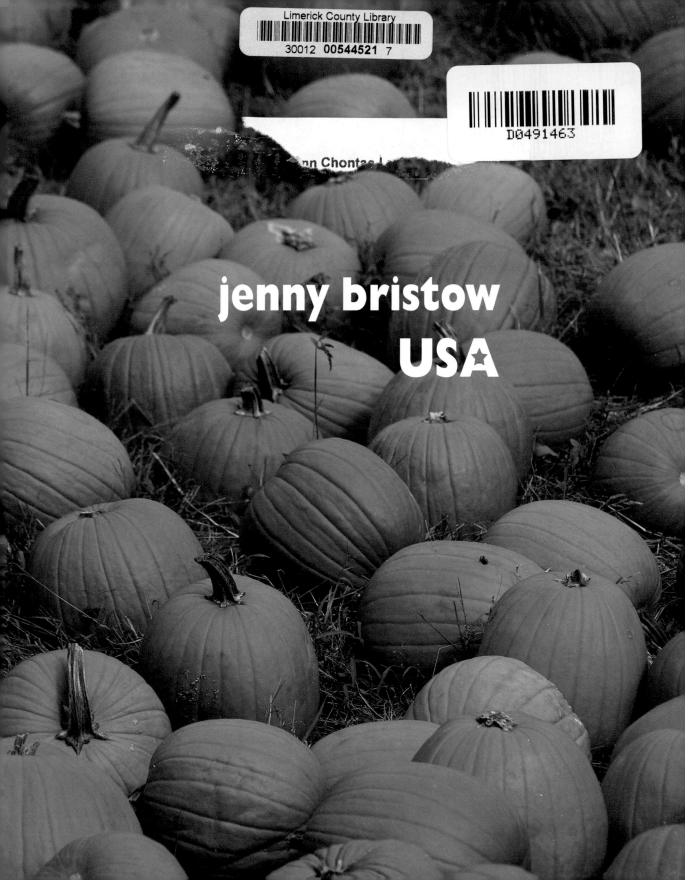

jenny bristow
USA

PRAISE FOR JENNY BRISTOW

'Her easy manner, gentle charm and clear, practical advice have made Jenny Bristow one of Ireland's favourite chefs.'
Belfast Telegraph

'The beauty of Jenny's style of cooking is its simplicity.'
Irish News

'As Ulster's answer to Delia Smith, Jenny has simply become a food phenomenon.'
Sunday World

'The term *joie de vivre* could have been created for Jenny Bristow.'
Ulster Tatler

jenny
bristow
USA ★

BLACKSTAFF
PRESS

BELFAST

IN ASSOCIATION WITH UTV

contents

mains

thanksgiving and christmas

desserts

baking

conversion tables

volume

1 tsp	5ml
1 dsp	10ml
1 tbsp	15ml
55ml	2floz
75ml	3floz
125ml	4floz
150ml	$1/4$pt
275ml	$1/2$pt
425ml	$3/4$pt
570ml	1pt
1 litre	$1^3/4$pt

oven temperatures

degrees centigrade	gas mark
140°	1
150°	2
170°	3
180°	4
190°	5
200°	6
220°	7
230°	8
240°	9

weights

grams	ounces
10g	$1/2$oz
25g	1oz
40g	$1^1/2$oz
50g	2oz
60g	$2^1/2$oz
75g	3oz
110g	4oz
125g	$4^1/2$oz
150g	5oz
175g	6oz
200g	7oz
225g	8oz
250g	9oz
275g	10oz
350g	12oz
400g	14oz
450g	1lb
700g	$1^1/2$lb
900g	2lb
1.3kg	3lb
1.8kg	4lb
2.3kg	5lb

measurements

millimetres	inches
3mm	$1/8$in
5mm	$1/4$in
1cm	$1/2$in
2cm	$3/4$in
2.5cm	1in
3cm	$1^1/4$in
4cm	$1^1/2$in
4.5cm	$1^3/4$in
5cm	2in
7.5cm	3in
10cm	4in
13cm	5in
15cm	6in
18cm	7in
20cm	8in
23cm	9in
25cm	10in
28cm	11in
30cm	12in

I have always drawn inspiration for my cooking from the places that I have visited, and I love bringing a little of the flavour of my travels back home. When I visited New England I was struck by the similarities between the American and Irish culinary traditions. Like us, New Englanders have a great passion for food, and a wonderful tradition of home cooking and baking.

While I was over in the US, I found masses of new ideas for pies and cakes, all with an American twist, and I couldn't resist including all my favourites in this book. Why not try apple-maple pandowdy as a change from crumble for Sunday lunch, or, if you're looking for a treat to have with a cup of coffee, try nutty squash and banana loaf or some buttermilk biscuits.

New England also provided me with endless ideas for first courses, snacks and mains. The recipes for seafood chowder and Boston scrod will let you sample some of New England's most popular seafood specialities, and dishes such as maple pork stew, cider-baked ham with oven-roasted squash, and hickory-smoked ribs are rich with the flavours of the area.

As you know, I believe that if you eat well, you feel well, which is why I have included my take on fast food, including mixed-grain pizza and home-made burgers, and a recipe for delicious baked beans.

The highlight of my stay in New England was Thanksgiving. The dishes served for this holiday have so much in common with our Christmas fare, so whether you are going to celebrate Thanksgiving – what better way to brighten up November? – or looking for new ideas for Christmas, you will love the section dedicated to these very special times of year. It's packed with everything you need, from the best way to cook your turkey to fresh new ideas for sauces, stuffings and vegetables.

And of course I haven't forgotten dessert – there's a wonderful Irish-American Christmas pudding with cranberries, blueberries and bourbon; pumpkin pie; blueberry trifle; and a fantastic recipe for poached pears, stuffed with walnuts, brown sugar and cinnamon.

These are the kinds of recipes that I love to cook at home for family and friends – they're quick and easy to prepare, and there's something suitable for every occasion. I hope that this book becomes a firm favourite in your kitchen.

Jenny Bristow

Deep-sea fishing in Gloucester, Massachusetts

brunch

Enjoying a visit to downtown Boston

A quick and nutritious breakfast for days when you are in a hurry.

breakfast
in a glass

570ml/1pt pink grapefruit juice
1 pink grapefruit – peeled and cut
   into segments
425ml/³/4pt natural Greek yoghurt

4 tbsp honey
2 tbsp wheatgerm oil
1 dsp granola (see page 14) or muesli

Whizz all the ingredients, except the granola, together in a blender for 30 seconds. Pour into tall glasses and serve with a sprinkle of granola or muesli over the top of each one.

The Swiss doctor Maximilian Bircher-Benner created this type of muesli at the turn of the last century – it's an original health food!

seasonal fruit
and yoghurt
bircher muesli

serves 4–6

225g/8oz rolled oats
125ml/4floz full-cream or semi-skimmed milk
1 apple – coarsely grated
2–3 pears – cored and sliced, or 2–3 plums
   or peaches – stoned and sliced
juice of ¹/2 lemon
5 dsp maple syrup or honey

275ml/¹/2pt natural or fruit-flavoured
   yoghurt
50g/2oz seedless grapes
1 banana – sliced
225g/8oz-can crushed pineapple –
   drained (optional)

Place the oats in a bowl, pour over the milk and leave to soak for around 10 minutes. Prepare the apple and pears (if using) and toss with the lemon juice immediately to prevent discoloration. Add to the oats with 4 dessertspoonfuls of the maple syrup or honey, the yoghurt, grapes and banana. If you are using plums or peaches or the canned pineapple, you should add them now too. Serve in individual bowls. Drizzle a little of the remaining maple syrup or honey over the top of each one.

I'm a great fan of a cup of tea and am always keen to try different kinds. This delicious iced mint tea is one of my favourites — best drunk out of doors in the sunshine.

iced mint tea

serves 2–3

6–8 sprigs of fresh mint – roughly chopped
1 tsp caster sugar
1 slice lemon

570ml/1pt boiling water
3–4 sprigs of fresh mint to garnish

Place the mint, caster sugar and lemon in a large bowl. Pour over the boiling water and leave to infuse for 15–20 minutes. Strain into a large jug, leave to cool, then chill. Serve over crushed ice in tall glasses, and garnish with sprigs of fresh mint.

Here is a really simple idea for a drink that can be made with apricots, peaches, nectarines or mangoes. Use a mixture of all four, or choose your favourite.

sparkling peach lemonade

serves 2–3

50g/2oz caster sugar
juice of 2 large oranges
grated zest of 1/2 orange
450g/1lb apricots, peaches, nectarines or mangoes
  – stoned and diced (skin the mangoes, if using)

570ml/1pt sparkling mineral water
1 orange – sliced
1 lemon – sliced

Place the sugar, orange juice and orange zest in a saucepan. Bring to the boil and simmer gently until the sugar has dissolved. Leave to cool. Whizz the soft fruit that you are using in a blender until puréed but retaining a little texture. Mix the fruit purée and sugar syrup together. Chill.

When ready to serve, add the sparkling water to the fruit mixture and stir well. Serve in tall glasses over crushed ice, garnished with slices of orange and lemon.

Granola is a great American favourite, made from oats, seeds and dried fruits. Try it as an alternative to muesli, or use it to make this delicious brunch recipe.

home-made granola
with maple yoghurt
and berries

makes about 800g/1³/4lb granola

450g/1lb rolled oats
2 tbsp sunflower oil
2 tbsp honey
1 tsp natural vanilla extract
75g/3oz flaked almonds
50g/2oz sesame seeds
50g/2oz flaxseeds
50g/2oz sunflower seeds
110g/4oz dried cranberries or raisins

maple yoghurt
125ml/4floz low-fat natural yoghurt
2 dsp maple syrup

berries
110g/4oz assorted fresh berries

Preheat the oven to 180°C/gas mark 4. Place the rolled oats in a large roasting tin and toast in the oven for approximately 15 minutes, turning once or twice during cooking.

In a small saucepan combine the oil, honey and vanilla extract, and heat until warm. Add the almonds, sesame seeds, flaxseeds and sunflower seeds to the honey mixture and stir. Remove the pan from the heat, and pour the honey and seeds over the oats. Mix well.

Continue to bake the coated oats for another 15 minutes, until browned and crisp, turning every 5 minutes so that they brown evenly. Break up the oat mixture into chunks with a wooden spoon and add the dried cranberries or raisins. Leave to cool completely. When cold, store in an airtight jar – the granola will keep in a cool place for 2–3 months.

To serve, combine the yoghurt and maple syrup. Take two glasses and spoon 2–3 dsp of granola into the bottom of each one. Add a layer of yoghurt and then top with a spoonful of berries.

Muffins are a staple of American eating, and are almost as popular here. This lovely recipe is inspired by some muffins I tried in New England.

cranberry, apple and sour cream muffins

makes 8–10

225g/8oz plain flour
1 tsp baking powder
1/2 tsp bicarbonate of soda
1 tsp ground cinnamon
1 tsp freshly grated nutmeg
1/2 tsp ground cloves

110g/4oz cranberries
1 Bramley apple – peeled, cored and chopped
50g/2oz caster sugar
2 eggs – beaten
110g/4oz butter – melted
150ml/1/4pt sour cream

Preheat the oven to 180°C/gas mark 4. Lightly grease a muffin pan or line with paper cases – the mixture will make 8–10 muffins.

Sift together the flour, baking powder, bicarbonate of soda and spices. Make a well in the centre of the dry mixture. Add the cranberries, apples and sugar. Pour in the eggs, butter and sour cream. Lightly mix the wet ingredients, then quickly stir in the flour mixture. Do not overmix – it does not matter if there are some floury patches. Spoon the mixture into the prepared muffin pans.

Bake the muffins for 15–20 minutes, until well risen, browned and springy to the touch. When cooked, wrap in a tea towel and allow to cool.

A great toasted sandwich if you like your food on the go!
This can be made with any kind of bread you like: wheaten,
bagels or – my favourite – walnut bread.

toasted winter
breakfast sandwich

serves 2

4 slices bread, or 2 bagels – halved
4 rindless rashers maple-cured bacon
175g/6oz cream cheese

$^1/_4$ tsp ground cinnamon
few drops of natural vanilla extract
1 dsp maple syrup or honey – warmed

Preheat the grill to its hottest setting. Toast the slices of bread or bagel halves
until lightly browned. Cook the bacon under the grill until crisp.

Meanwhile, in a bowl, mix the cream cheese, cinnamon and vanilla. Spread the
toasted bread with the cream cheese mixture. Top two slices or bagel halves
with the bacon. Flash under a hot grill for 30 seconds, then top with the
other remaining toast or bagel halves. Press well together, cut in half and
serve the sandwiches as they are, or with a little maple syrup or honey
drizzled over the top.

A real treat – these pancakes are perfect for a special brunch. For a lighter version, serve the pancakes with yoghurt instead of honeycomb butter.

blueberry buttermilk
pancakes
with honeycomb butter

makes 8–10 pancakes

150g/5oz self-raising flour
pinch of salt
grated zest of 1 lemon
25g/1oz caster sugar
3 egg yolks
25g/1oz butter – softened
275ml/¹/₂pt buttermilk
1 tsp lemon juice
110g/4oz blueberries – plus extra
   to serve (optional)

2 egg whites – whisked until stiff
small knob of butter for cooking

honeycomb butter
50g/2oz honeycomb
110g/4oz unsalted butter
1 tsp maple syrup

Prepare the honeycomb butter well in advance. Crush the honeycomb using a pestle and mortar, or in a plastic bag with a rolling pin, until smooth. Pour into a bowl. Add the softened butter and maple syrup and mix well. Transfer the butter to a rectangle of greaseproof paper, and shape it into a log. Allow to firm up in the fridge before slicing into rounds.

Sieve the flour into a bowl and mix in the salt, lemon zest and sugar. Make a well in the flour and add the egg yolks and softened butter. Begin to add the buttermilk a little at a time, stirring gently, and gradually mixing in the flour to make a smooth, thick batter. Add the lemon juice. Gently fold in the blueberries and the egg whites, taking care not to knock the air out of the mixture.

To cook, melt the knob of butter in a non-stick frying pan. When the butter starts to sizzle, reduce the temperature and drop 2 dessertspoonfuls of the batter into the pan to form a small pancake. Cook for approximately 2 minutes, until the underside of the pancake is golden and the top is just set. Turn and cook the other side until it is golden also. Transfer to a plate and keep warm. Repeat until all the batter is used.

Serve the warm pancakes with slices of honeycomb butter and extra blueberries, if liked.

This is a great breakfast-time treat, and you can vary the flavour by choosing different kinds of marmalade. My favourite is a combination of lemon, lime and orange. These French toast sandwiches are delicious with a pot of freshly brewed coffee.

citrus marmalade
french toast

serves 2

225g/8oz cream cheese
grated zest of 1 small orange
1 tsp demerara sugar
4 dsp marmalade
8 slices fruit loaf or currant bread

3 large eggs
125ml/4floz milk
$1/4$ tsp freshly grated nutmeg
small knob of butter for cooking

In a bowl, beat together the cream cheese, orange zest, sugar and marmalade. Spread four of the slices of bread with the marmalade mixture. Top with the remaining slices of bread and press down well.

Beat together the eggs, milk and nutmeg in a large shallow bowl. In a large frying pan, heat the butter until hot and sizzling. Dip the sandwiches into the egg mixture, turning to ensure that each side is thoroughly coated. Do not leave them in the egg for too long or they will become soggy and difficult to handle. Add the sandwiches to the pan and cook for 4–5 minutes on each side, until golden and crisp. Drain on kitchen paper and serve hot, cut into fingers or wedges.

I love this combination – the tartness of the orange and cranberry sauce with the sweetness of the marmalade-filled French toast.

french toast
with cranberry and
orange sauce

serves 2

4 slices thick crusty bread
25g/1oz butter – softened
4 dsp marmalade
3 large eggs
275ml/1/2pt milk or cream
small knob of butter for cooking

sauce
110g/4oz fresh or frozen cranberries
grated zest of 1 orange
juice of 1 clementine (approximately 2–3 tbsp)
1/4 tsp ground cinnamon
25g/1oz soft brown sugar
4 dsp water

Make the sauce before cooking the French toast: heat the cranberries, orange zest, clementine juice, cinnamon, sugar and water in a saucepan until boiling. Reduce the heat and cook gently for 6–8 minutes until the cranberries soften and burst. If you like smooth sauce, blend in a food processor. Set to one side and keep warm.

Spread one side of each slice of bread with softened butter and marmalade, and sandwich together.

Beat together the eggs and milk or cream in a large shallow bowl. Heat the butter in a large frying pan until hot and sizzling. Dip the sandwiches into the egg mixture, turning to ensure that each side is thoroughly coated. Do not leave the sandwiches in the egg for too long or they will become soggy and difficult to handle. Add the sandwiches to the pan and cook for 4–5 minutes on each side, until golden and crisp. Drain on kitchen paper and serve hot with the sauce.

A delicious change from the usual breakfast fare, these fritters are an American classic.

sweetcorn fritters
with cranberry and chilli ketchup

serves 4

225g/8oz canned sweetcorn kernels, or 2 large
  cobs if using fresh
1/2 small red or white onion – finely chopped
1 dsp chopped fresh parsley
1 dsp chopped fresh coriander
110g/4oz plain flour
salt and freshly ground black pepper
1 heaped tsp baking powder
2 large eggs – lightly beaten
2 tbsp milk
olive or sunflower oil for cooking
4–6 rindless rashers maple-cured streaky bacon

8–10 baby tomatoes
1 tsp balsamic vinegar

ketchup
450g/1lb fresh cranberries, or frozen cranberries –
  thoroughly defrosted
110g/4oz soft brown sugar
125ml/4floz cider vinegar
2 red chillies – deseeded and finely chopped,
  or 2 dsp chilli sauce
1/2 red onion – finely chopped

Make the ketchup first: place the cranberries, sugar, vinegar, chillies or chilli sauce and onion in a saucepan. Heat together for 15–20 minutes, stirring occasionally, but do not allow to bubble too rapidly. If you like smooth ketchup, blend in a food processor. Set to one side and keep warm.

If using fresh sweetcorn, boil or steam the cobs for 8–10 minutes. Cool, and scrape off the kernels using a sharp knife.

Place the corn in a bowl with the onion, parsley and coriander.

Make the batter by sifting the flour, salt, pepper and baking powder into another bowl. Make a well in the centre, add the egg and half the milk. Gradually mix the flour into the egg. The batter will still be quite stiff, so add the remainder of the milk. Stir in the sweetcorn mixture.

Heat a little oil in a shallow frying pan. Add 2 dessertspoonfuls of batter. Cook for approximately 2 minutes until the underside of the fritter is golden, then turn over and cook the other side until it is golden also. Drain on kitchen paper and keep warm. Repeat until all the batter is used.

Preheat a griddle pan. Place the bacon rashers and tomatoes on the griddle pan. Sprinkle with the balsamic vinegar and cook for 2–3 minutes, until the bacon is crispy and the tomatoes are slightly blackened. Serve immediately with the sweetcorn fritters, and cranberry and chilli ketchup.

I love the flavour of this jam – the combination of autumn fruits just works a treat.

apple, pear and plum jam

makes approximately 2.7kg/6lb

1.3kg/3lb granulated or preserving sugar
450g/1lb eating apples – peeled, cored and diced
450g/1lb pears – peeled, cored and diced
450g/1lb plums – stoned and diced
grated zest of 2 lemons

5cm/2in piece of fresh root ginger – peeled and grated
150ml/$^1/_4$ pint of water
1–2 cinnamon sticks – broken in half

Preheat the oven to 190°C/gas mark 5. Spread the sugar on a baking tray or roasting tin and place in the oven for 10–12 minutes to warm through.

While the sugar is warming, put the apples, pears, plums, lemon zest and ginger in a large pan and add the water. Heat, stirring, until the water boils and then reduce the heat. Cover and simmer gently for 15–20 minutes, until the fruit is soft and tender. The ripeness of the fruit will determine the time required – if the fruit is ripe then it will soften more quickly.

Turn off the heat under the pan and add the warmed sugar. Stir until it has dissolved. Add the cinnamon sticks. Turn on the heat again, keeping it as low as possible for a moment or two, stirring to ensure that the sugar has completely dissolved. Then increase the heat and bring the jam to the boil. Cook for 10–15 minutes.

To test if the jam is ready, take it off the heat, spoon a little onto a chilled saucer and let it cool for a few seconds. Push it with your finger – if the surface of the jam wrinkles, the setting point has been reached. If not, boil for a further 5 minutes and test again. Carefully pour the boiling hot jam into warmed sterilised jars (see page 123) and immediately cover with waxed discs and airtight lids. If you pot and cover the jam as soon as it is ready, it should keep for months in a cool, dark cupboard.

Weigh the pumpkin and pineapple after you have prepared them as the skin, seeds and core vary in weight. Pineapple brings a fabulous, fresh flavour to rich, smooth pumpkin in this unusual jam.

pumpkin and pineapple jam

makes approximately 2.7kg/6lb

900g–1.3kg/2–3lb prepared pumpkin or squash
flesh – cut into 1.5cm/^{1}/2in chunks
450g/1lb prepared fresh pineapple –
cut into 1.5cm/^{1}/2in chunks
900g–1.3kg/2–3lb granulated sugar

Place the pumpkin and pineapple in a large stainless steel pan, sprinkle the sugar over the top and leave to sit for up to 1 hour, if possible, to draw out the juices from the ingredients.

Place the pan on the heat and heat slowly, stirring to ensure the sugar has completely dissolved. Then bring to the boil. Boil rapidly for 15–20 minutes.

To test if the jam is ready, take it off the heat, spoon a little liquid onto a chilled saucer and let it cool for a few seconds. Push it with your finger – if the surface of the jam wrinkles, the setting point has been reached. If not, boil for a further 5 minutes and test again. Carefully pour the boiling hot jam into warmed sterilised jars (see page 123) and immediately cover with waxed discs and airtight lids. If you pot and cover the jam as soon as it is ready, it should keep for months in a cool, dark cupboard.

first courses and fast food

Visiting the Haymarket in Boston

Both tasty and nutritious, this hearty soup is a meal on its own.

pasta, lentil and
chorizo soup

400g/14oz-can lentils (Puy, red or any other kind) – drained
3 bay leaves – creased in half
2 dsp chopped fresh coriander
275ml/1/2pt vegetable or chicken stock
1 dsp olive oil

1 large onion – finely chopped
400g/14oz-can chopped tomatoes
110g/4oz macaroni
110g/4oz chorizo, sliced
6–8 fresh basil leaves – torn

Place the lentils, bay leaves and coriander in a saucepan. Stir in the stock and cover the pan, then simmer for 10 minutes.

In a separate saucepan, heat the olive oil, add the onion and cook over a gentle heat for 5–6 minutes until it is soft but not coloured.

Meanwhile cook the macaroni in a saucepan of boiling water for 6–7 minutes, or until just tender.

Purée the lentil mixture in a food processor or blender, and then add it to the onions. Stir in the tomatoes and chorizo. Bring to the boil, then reduce the heat and simmer gently for 5–6 minutes. Stir in the cooked, drained macaroni, bring back to a simmer, sprinkle with the torn basil leaves and serve immediately.

This soup makes the most of two of autumn's finest ingredients. The slow-roasted squash and apple combine with the spicy flavour of cider (or apple juice) to make a warming and delicious first course or light lunch.

roasted apple and
butternut squash
soup

serves 6–8

3 large cooking apples (450g/1lb) – peeled, cored and halved

900g/2lb prepared butternut squash flesh – cut into large chunks

2 onions – cut into chunks

2 carrots – cut into chunks

3 cloves garlic – finely chopped

1 tsp fresh rosemary – chopped

1/2 tsp ground ginger

1/2 tsp ground mace

25g/1oz soft brown sugar

25g/1oz butter or 1 dsp olive oil

4–6 tbsp water

570ml/1pt vegetable or chicken stock

275ml/1/2pt cider or unsweetened apple juice

salt and freshly ground black pepper

horseradish cream

2 tsp horseradish sauce or grated fresh horseradish

2 tsp natural yoghurt

Preheat the oven to 200°C/gas mark 6. Place the apples, squash, onions, carrots, garlic, rosemary, ginger, mace and sugar in a roasting tin. Mix well. Dot with the butter or drizzle with oil and sprinkle the water over the top. Cover with foil and roast until all the vegetables have softened, approximately 1–1 1/2 hours.

Scoop some of the vegetables from the roasting tin and place in a food processor. Add some of the stock and purée until smooth, then pour into a large saucepan. Repeat until all the vegetables have been puréed.

Stir in the remainder of the stock and the cider or apple juice and bring to the boil. Reduce the heat and simmer gently for 10–15 minutes to blend the flavours. Season to taste.

Meanwhile, in a separate bowl, mix the horseradish sauce or grated horseradish with the yoghurt.

Ladle the soup into warmed bowls and swirl a little horseradish cream into each one. Serve immediately.

Seafood chowder is a traditional and enormously popular soup throughout New England. It's often made with clams but I have used cockles and mussels, which are equally delicious and much easier to find.

seafood
chowder

50g/2oz butter

110g/4oz salt pork or thick-cut rindless streaky bacon – chopped

2 garlic cloves – finely chopped

1 onion – finely chopped

4 celery stalks – finely diced

25g/1oz plain flour

275ml/1/2pt milk

570ml/1pt cooking liquid from cockles and mussels

450g/1lb potatoes – diced

1 tsp dried thyme

2–3 bay leaves – creased in half

1 tbsp finely chopped fresh parsley

1 tbsp finely chopped fresh coriander

dash of Tabasco

dash of Worcestershire sauce

450g/1lb cockles – cooked and shelled (see page 122)

450g/1lb mussels – cooked and shelled (see page 122)

275ml/1/2pt whipping or double cream

salt and freshly ground black pepper

In a large pan, melt the butter and cook the salt pork or streaky bacon until crisp, without letting the butter discolour or burn. Use a draining spoon to remove the pork or bacon from the pan. Add the garlic, onion and celery to the butter in the pan and cook for 3–4 minutes until they begin to soften. Again, do not let the butter burn as this will spoil the flavour of the chowder.

In a small bowl, blend the flour with a little of the milk until smooth. Add the blended flour mixture and the remainder of the milk to the vegetables, stirring. Add the shellfish cooking liquid, potatoes, thyme and bay leaves. Bring to the boil, stirring all the time. Reduce the heat and add half of the parsley, half of the coriander, the Tabasco and Worcestershire sauce.

Simmer gently for 6–7 minutes until the potatoes are cooked. Stir in the cockles and mussels and heat through. Then stir in the cream and heat without boiling. Add seasoning to taste and ladle into warmed bowls.

Sprinkle the cooked salt pork or bacon over the top, garnish with the remainder of the parsley and coriander, and serve with crusty bread.

The coating on these crab cakes adds a wonderful crunch — and it is good for you too. Flaxseeds are available in all good healthfood shops and in some supermarkets.

cape cod
crab cakes

serves 4

450g/1lb crab meat — fresh, canned, or frozen and thawed
50g/2oz fresh breadcrumbs
2 spring onions — very finely chopped
1/2 red pepper — deseeded and very finely chopped
2 tbsp finely chopped fresh parsley, coriander or dill

1/2 tsp paprika
grated zest and juice of 1/2 lemon
1 egg
1 egg yolk
50g/2oz flaxseeds
50g/2oz breadcrumbs
25g/1oz butter
1 dsp olive oil

In a large bowl, mix the crab meat, breadcrumbs, spring onions, red pepper, parsley or other herbs, paprika and lemon zest and juice. Beat the egg with the egg yolk and pour into the mixture. Stir well to bind the ingredients together.

In a bowl, mix the breadcrumbs and flaxseeds for coating, then place in a thick layer on a plate.

Shape a quarter of the crab mixture into a cake and coat well with the flaxseed mixture. Repeat with the remaining mixture to make a total of four crab cakes.

Heat the butter and oil in a large frying pan. Add the crab cakes and cook for about 2 minutes on each side, until golden brown and crisp. When cooked, drain on kitchen paper and serve with ancho-chilli mayo (see opposite). If necessary, cook the crab cakes in two batches, keeping the first pair warm until the second two are cooked.

This spicy mayo is great with crab cakes (see opposite), hamburgers (see page 44), or as a dip with potato wedges.

ancho-chilli mayo

serves 4

1/2 red pepper – deseeded
1 ancho chilli (see page 122) – deseeded
  and chopped
1 garlic clove – finely chopped
1 dsp olive oil

1 dsp lemon juice
1/2 tsp paprika
dash of Tabasco
125ml/4floz mayonnaise
1 spring onion – finely chopped

Preheat the grill to its hottest setting. Grill the pepper, skin side up, until slightly blackened and soft. Peel off the skin and leave to cool. Place the pepper in a blender. Add the chilli, garlic, olive oil, lemon juice, paprika and Tabasco, and whizz briefly, until the ingredients are well mixed but still have some texture.

Place the mayonnaise in a bowl. Add the pepper mixture and spring onions. Mix well and serve.

This quick pickle is delicious with cold roast meat and fish.

sweet pickled cucumber

serves 4

1 cucumber – finely sliced
salt and freshly ground black pepper
1 red onion – diced

25g/1oz caster sugar
2 tbsp rice wine vinegar
1 tbsp finely chopped fresh dill or fennel

Place the cucumber in a colander and sprinkle with a little salt. Leave for 10–15 minutes, then rinse thoroughly.

In a bowl mix the cucumber, onion, sugar, vinegar and dill or fennel. Season to taste. Chill for at least one hour before serving.

This is my US-inspired take on the traditional prawn cocktail – healthier, lighter and, I think, even more delicious.

seafood
margarita

225g/8oz peeled, cooked jumbo prawns
110g/4oz crab meat – fresh, canned, or frozen and thawed
1/2 yellow pepper – deseeded and finely sliced
1/4 small red onion – finely sliced
1/2 mango – peeled, stoned and diced
1 tbsp chopped fresh coriander

dressing
2 dsp lime juice
1 dsp olive oil
1 tsp English mustard
1 tsp Tabasco
freshly ground black pepper

to serve
mixed salad leaves
1 lime – cut into wedges

Mix the prawns, crab, pepper, onion, mango and a sprinkle of the coriander (reserve some for the dressing).

In a small bowl, make the dressing by mixing the lime juice, olive oil, remaining coriander, mustard, Tabasco and black pepper. Pour the dressing over the prawns and crab meat. Toss and allow the flavours to infuse for 15 minutes before serving.

To serve, place a few salad leaves in each of the bowls. Spoon the seafood mixture on top. Garnish with wedges of lime on the side.

Pizza is one of the world's most popular fast foods. Here is my healthy version, which has a scone-type base — much quicker to prepare than a traditional yeast-based one. The toppings work really well together — but the base will go with any of your favourite meats, cheeses or herbs.

mixed-grain pizza
with prosciutto, mozzarella and pesto

serves 6–8

50g/2oz plain flour
50g/2oz polenta or cornmeal
50g/2oz wholemeal flour
1 tsp bicarbonate of soda
salt and freshly ground black pepper
150ml/¼pt buttermilk

1–2 dsp olive oil
3 tbsp sun-dried tomato paste
225g/8oz cherry tomatoes – halved
110g/4oz mozzarella cheese – sliced
225g/8oz prosciutto
1 dsp pesto

Preheat the oven to 200°C/gas mark 6. Grease a baking sheet.

In a large bowl, combine the plain flour, polenta, wholemeal flour, bicarbonate of soda, salt and black pepper. Add the buttermilk a little at a time and mix to a soft dough.

Turn out the dough onto a surface dusted with a little flour and roll into a thin rectangle, approximately 25x15cm/10x6in. Place on the baking sheet and brush with olive oil. Spread with the sun-dried tomato paste, and arrange the tomatoes and two-thirds of the mozzarella on top.

Bake the pizza for about 12–15 minutes until lightly browned and cooked. Arrange the prosciutto and remaining cheese on the pizza. Dot with the pesto and return to the oven for a further 3–4 minutes. Serve immediately, with a mixed leaf salad.

I think that this lovely salad is best served warm, with the blue cheese just beginning to melt.

winter salad

450g/1lb prepared butternut squash or pumpkin flesh – cut into chunks
1 small red onion – finely sliced
2–3 dsp olive oil
1 dsp balsamic vinegar
2 dsp honey
25g/1oz butter – melted
50g/2oz couscous
125ml/4floz hot chicken or vegetable stock

110g/4oz Ballyblue cheese – cubed
25g/1oz walnuts – coarsely chopped
1 dsp chopped fresh herbs (e.g. chives, parsley, coriander)
salt and freshly ground black pepper

dressing
6 tbsp olive oil
2 tbsp cider vinegar
1/2 tsp English mustard

Preheat the oven to 200°C/gas mark 6. Place the squash or pumpkin and onion in a roasting dish with the oil, vinegar, honey and butter. Mix well and then roast in the oven for 20 minutes, turning occasionally.

Meanwhile place the couscous in a bowl and pour over the hot stock. Stir well then cover. Leave to stand for around 10 minutes. Fork through the couscous to separate the grains.

Make the dressing by whisking all the oil, vinegar and mustard together in a bowl.

Add the Ballyblue cheese, walnuts, herbs and couscous to the roasting tin. Pour over the dressing, mix well, season to taste and serve.

The walnuts in this salad take a little time to prepare but you will soon see why they are worth the effort!

smoked salmon salad
with raspberry vinaigrette and spiced walnuts

serves 3–4

1 cos lettuce
225g/8oz smoked salmon
110g/4oz Ballyblue cheese – crumbled

1 tsp Dijon mustard
150ml/^{1}/4pt grapeseed oil
freshly ground black pepper

raspberry vinaigrette

150ml/^{1}/4pt red wine vinegar
110g/4oz raspberries
1 tbsp spring onions – finely chopped
1 tbsp maple syrup
1 tbsp lemon juice

spiced walnuts

225g/8oz walnuts
110g/4oz granulated sugar
1 tsp paprika
1 tsp cumin
1 tbsp olive oil

First prepare the raspberry vinaigrette: in a small saucepan, heat the vinegar, raspberries and spring onions for 2–3 minutes. Strain, retaining only the vinegar. Reheat the vinegar with the maple syrup and lemon juice. Simmer for a couple of minutes, then pour into a bowl. Whisk in the mustard, oil and pepper. Leave to cool and then chill until you assemble the salad.

Next make the spiced walnuts. Place the walnuts in a pan and cover with water. Bring to the boil then simmer hard for 5–6 minutes. Drain thoroughly in a sieve. Mix the sugar, paprika and cumin in a small bowl and toss the walnuts in this mixture. Set aside to dry for 10–15 minutes.

Heat the oil in a frying pan and fry the walnuts until they are caramel-coloured and crisp. They will burn easily, so keep turning them and do not allow them to overcook. Using a draining spoon, remove them from the pan as soon as they are ready.

To assemble the salad, tear the lettuce leaves into large pieces and arrange on a plate. Lay the smoked salmon over the lettuce, pour over the raspberry vinaigrette and scatter the cheese and spiced walnuts on top. Serve immediately.

This is a versatile recipe – ideal as a first course, and great as part of a barbecue or picnic.

roasted garlic
cheesecakes
with mediterranean salad

serves 6

3–4 sheets filo pastry
25g/1oz butter – melted
225g/8oz cream cheese
2 eggs – lightly beaten
1 egg yolk
2 dsp whipping cream
salt and freshly ground black pepper

roasted garlic
1 bulb garlic
1 tbsp olive oil

salad
110g/4oz black olives – pitted and chopped
110g/4oz feta cheese – cubed
110g/4oz sun-blush tomatoes – chopped

Preheat the oven to 200°C/gas mark 6. Prepare the garlic first. Cut the very top off the bulb of garlic. Place the bulb on a square of foil and sprinkle with the olive oil. Enclose the garlic completely in the foil and place on a baking sheet or in an ovenproof dish. Roast for 25–30 minutes, until the garlic is soft. Leave to cool. When cool enough to handle, squeeze the soft flesh from each clove into a saucer or bowl. Set aside.

Reduce the oven temperature to 190°C/gas mark 5. Brush each sheet of filo pastry liberally with melted butter, layering them one on top of the other on a board. Cut the stack of sheets into quarters and use each quarter to line a hole in a patty tin, Yorkshire pudding tin or deep muffin tin.

Beat the cream cheese until softened. Then mix in the eggs and egg yolk a little at a time until combined. Stir in the cream, seasoning and garlic. Spoon this mixture carefully into the filo cases and bake for 12–15 minutes, until the pastry is golden brown and the filling has set.

Meanwhile, to make the salad, mix the olives, feta and tomatoes.

Serve the cheesecakes, hot or cold, with the Mediterranean salad and mixed leaves.

I love the combination of flavours in this dish — sharp, spicy chilli with sweet maple syrup.

maple-glazed
chicken wings

serves 8

900g/2lb chicken wings
1 large onion – finely chopped
150ml/^{1}/4pt maple syrup
2 tbsp cider vinegar

^{1}/2 tsp mustard
4 tbsp chilli sauce
1 tsp Worcestershire sauce

In a large bowl (big enough to hold the chicken wings), mix the onion, maple syrup, cider vinegar, mustard, chilli sauce and Worcestershire sauce. Add the chicken wings, turning them in the marinade to coat each one thoroughly. Cover and leave in a cool place for 1–1^1/2 hours. The chicken can be marinated for longer, in which case it should be placed in the fridge.

Preheat the oven to 200°C/gas mark 6. Transfer the wings to a large ovenproof dish and bake for 20–25 minutes, turning occasionally, until they are golden and thoroughly cooked. Serve with crusty bread and a green salad.

corn on the cob
with seasoned butter

serves 4

Simply boil four cobs in salted water for 8–10 minutes, or until tender, and serve with one of these flavoured butters.

chilli butter
Mix 50g/2oz butter with 1 tsp chilli powder.

pecan butter
Mix 50g/2oz butter with 25g/1oz finely chopped pecan nuts.

lime and peppercorn
Mix 50g/2oz butter with 1 tsp crushed pink or black peppercorns and the grated zest and juice of half a lime.

This sandwich may take a little more time to prepare than a standard one, but it's definitely worth it. Chicken, bacon and cheese is a fantastic combination, but you can also experiment with your favourite ingredients.

country club
chicken sandwich

serves 1

2 dsp olive oil
1 chicken breast fillet – cut into broad strips
4 rashers maple-cure streaky bacon
2 thick slices ciabatta
1 clove garlic – finely chopped

2 tsp American-style mustard
4 slices smoked Applewood cheese
1 dsp finely chopped fresh coriander
1 tsp pesto

Heat a drizzle of the oil on a griddle pan. Add the chicken strips and bacon and cook, turning once or twice, until they are crisp and golden. Remove and keep warm.

Toast one side of each of the ciabatta slices on the griddle pan. Place them toasted sides up on a board. Combine the garlic and remaining olive oil, and brush over the toasted sides of the bread. Turn the bread over, and spread the untoasted sides with mustard. Place two slices of the cheese on top of the mustard, and add two rashers of bacon. Now add the chicken, the remaining bacon, coriander, pesto and the final two slices of cheese. Place the other slices of bread on top (untoasted side down) and press down well.

Reheat the sandwich for 2–3 minutes on each side on the griddle pan, until the cheese melts. Serve immediately. Boston baked beans (see opposite) and a few crisps are the perfect accompaniments.

Traditionally, Boston baked beans take hours to cook, but I have transformed this classic into a fast-food treat by using pre-cooked beans. The result is delicious and practical.

boston
baked beans

2 tbsp soft brown sugar
125ml/4floz dark molasses or treacle
1 tsp mustard
1 tbsp Worcestershire sauce
2 x 400g/14oz cans haricot beans – drained, liquid
  reserved

salt and freshly ground black pepper
$1/4$ tsp ground cinnamon
110g/4oz thick-cut rindless streaky
  bacon – chopped
$1/2$ onion – finely chopped
1 bay leaf – creased in half

Preheat the oven to 170°C/gas mark 3. In a large casserole dish, combine the sugar, molasses or treacle, mustard, Worcestershire sauce, 275ml/$1/2$pt of the reserved liquid from the beans, salt, pepper and cinnamon. Stir until thoroughly combined. Add the bacon, beans, onion and bay leaf. Mix well.

Cover and bake for 1 hour, stirring occasionally. If necessary, add a little more of the reserved liquid to prevent the beans from drying out during cooking. Serve hot, with the club sandwich (see opposite).

If you prefer, you can cook the beans on the hob instead of in the oven. Bring the liquid mixture to the boil first, then add the remaining ingredients. Reduce the heat so that the mixture simmers steadily, cover, and cook for about 30 minutes.

Hamburgers are always a big hit with everyone in the family, and it's so easy to make your own. Always try to use good-quality, locally reared beef.

home-style
hamburgers
with mushrooms

serves 4–5

450g/1lb minced steak
1 small red onion – finely chopped
1 tbsp chopped fresh herbs (e.g. parsley,
    chives, coriander)

^{1}/2 tsp English mustard
freshly ground black pepper
1 dsp olive oil
225g/8oz mushrooms – sliced

In a large bowl mix the minced steak with the onion, herbs, mustard and pepper. Shape the mixture into 4–5 burgers approximately 1cm/^{1}/2in thick. If you have time, chill them for 30 minutes or so as this will help them to hold their shape while cooking.

Heat the oil in a frying pan. Cook the burgers for 4–5 minutes on each side, until they are cooked through. Shortly before the burgers are ready, add the mushrooms to the pan and fry until golden brown.

Serve in buns with ancho-chilli mayo (see page 33).

This is one of my favourite dishes to serve as a snack or starter. It's quite rich, so follow it with something light.

salmon gratin

serves 6

175g/6oz fresh spinach
2–3 boiled potatoes – thinly sliced
110g/4oz smoked salmon
6–8 spring onions – finely chopped
freshly ground black pepper
juice of 1/2 lemon
150ml/1/4pt soured cream

sauce
25g/1oz butter
25g/1oz plain flour
570ml/1pt milk
2 egg yolks
110g/4oz mozzarella cheese
2 egg whites – whisked until stiff
2 tbsp Parmesan cheese – grated

Preheat the oven to 200°C/gas mark 6. Butter six small gratin dishes.

Wash the spinach and remove any tough stalks. Steam until just wilted, squeeze out any moisture and chop finely. Arrange the potatoes in the bottom of each gratin dish. Sprinkle some spring onions, pepper and lemon juice over each one. Add a layer of spinach and another of smoked salmon, again sprinkling each with spring onions, pepper and lemon juice. Using half of the soured cream, top each dish with a spoonful (the remainder goes into the sauce).

To make the sauce, melt the butter in a small saucepan, add the flour, and cook, stirring, for 1 minute. Remove from the heat and whisk in the milk, egg yolks, the remainder of the soured cream, and half of the mozzarella cheese. Finally fold in the whisked egg whites. Pour the sauce over the gratin dishes, sprinkle with the remaining mozzarella and Parmesan cheese, and bake for 10–15 minutes, until golden brown.

mains

Taking a break from fishing, out in the bay in Gloucester, Massachusetts

spice-crusted
turbot

2 tbsp coriander seeds
2 tbsp cumin seeds
1 tbsp sea salt or to taste
2–3 garlic cloves – finely chopped

$1/2$ tsp madras curry powder
freshly ground black pepper
2 portions fish fillet, such as turbot or cod
   (weighing approximately 110g/4oz each)
2 dsp sunflower oil

Roast the coriander and cumin seeds in a dry frying pan over a low to medium heat until they are aromatic and begin to pop. Pound the seeds, using a pestle and mortar, until fine. Mix with the salt, garlic, curry powder and pepper. Rub the flesh side of the fish fillets with this mixture.

In a large frying pan, heat the oil over a medium heat until it is just shimmering hot – before it begins to smoke. Add the fish, spiced side down, and sear for 1–2 minutes. Take care not to let the spices burn or they will become bitter. Turn and cook for a further 1–2 minutes, or until the fish is cooked through. Thicker fillets will take slightly longer to cook. Use a fish slice to transfer the fish to warm plates. Serve with chive mash (see opposite).

chive mash

6 potatoes diced
25g/1oz butter
4 dsp cream

salt and freshly ground black pepper
1 tbsp fresh chopped chives

Cook the potatoes in salted, boiling water for 12–15 minutes, until soft and tender. Drain and mash. Add the butter, cream, seasoning and chives. Mix well and serve hot.

A delightful sauce with loads of texture and flavour. It's particularly good with chicken and beef, or as a vegetarian dish served with rice.

mushroom ragout

1 tbsp olive oil
1 garlic clove – finely chopped
1 celery stalk – diced
1 small carrot – diced
1/2 small fennel bulb – diced

225g/8oz mushrooms – sliced
110g/4oz Puy lentils
salt and freshly ground black pepper
275ml/1/2pt vegetable stock
2 tsp soy sauce

Heat the oil in a large frying pan, add the garlic and cook for about 1 minute. Add the celery, carrot and fennel and cook for 2 minutes. Stir in the mushrooms and cook for an additional minute before adding the lentils, seasoning, stock and soy sauce. Bring to the boil, reduce the heat and cover. Simmer gently for 15–20 minutes or until the lentils are cooked. Serve hot.

Boston scrod is a simple fish dish, traditionally made with young cod. This is my slightly more elaborate version featuring cod, prawns and a sauce of cream, Parmesan and lemon juice – a stunning fish pie.

boston
scrod

serves 6

6 potatoes – cut into large chunks
450g/1lb cod fillet – skinned and boned
225g/8oz large peeled cooked prawns
50g/2oz butter
4 spring onions – roughly chopped
grated zest of 2 lemons
2 dsp coarsely chopped fresh parsley

150ml/¼pt single cream
juice of 1 lemon
450g/1lb fresh spinach – steamed until just wilted
1 dsp olive oil
175g/6oz breadcrumbs
110g/4oz Parmesan cheese shavings
lemon wedges, to serve

Preheat the oven to 190°C/gas mark 5. Grease a large ovenproof dish or pie dish.

Steam the potatoes for 12 minutes. Cut the fish into large chunks and place in the dish. Add the prawns.

Melt 25g/1oz of the butter in a pan. Add the spring onions, half the lemon zest, the parsley and cream. Cook gently without boiling for 1–2 minutes. Add the steamed potatoes and lemon juice. Remove from the heat and mix well.

Top the fish with the spinach, then pour over the potato mixture. Melt the remaining butter with the olive oil. Add the breadcrumbs and toss or stir lightly around so they absorb the oil and butter. Add the remainder of the lemon zest and two-thirds of the Parmesan shavings, then mix gently. Scatter the breadcrumb mixture over the top of the pie. Sprinkle with the remaining Parmesan cheese and bake for approximately 20 minutes, until crisp and golden.

Serve piping hot with the lemon wedges.

I firmly believe that the simplest way to cook fish is often the best. This is a recipe that I use all the time and it works brilliantly with most white fish, including cod, haddock, mullet and whiting. Choose whichever looks best at the fishmonger.

oven-roasted fish
with lemon, lime and parsley crust

serves 4

4 portions fish fillet (weighing
   approximately 110g/4oz each)
grated zest of 1 lemon
grated zest of 1 lime
1 tbsp fresh herbs (e.g. parsley) – chopped

2 garlic cloves – finely chopped
50g/2oz Parmesan cheese – grated
110g/4oz white breadcrumbs
2 dsp olive oil

Preheat the oven to 200°C/gas mark 6. Grease an ovenproof dish or tray. Place the fish fillets in the prepared dish.

In a bowl, mix the lemon zest, lime zest, herbs, garlic, Parmesan cheese, breadcrumbs and olive oil. Spread this mixture evenly over the top of the fish fillets. Bake in the oven for 15–17 minutes, until the fish is cooked and flakes easily. Thicker fillets will take longer to cook. Serve immediately.

A New England version of the classic French ratatouille, this is delicious served on its own, with bread, or over pasta, and also as a side dish with meat or fish.

ratatouille

serves 6–8

1 1/2 aubergines – roughly chopped
2 tsp salt
150ml/1/4pt olive oil
1 red onion – finely chopped
1 onion – finely chopped
4–5 garlic cloves – finely chopped
2–3 tbsp chopped fresh oregano
3–4 tbsp chopped fresh flat-leaf parsley

salt and freshly ground black pepper
2–3 dsp tomato purée
450g/1lb prepared pumpkin or butternut squash flesh – diced
225g/8oz courgettes – diced
1 red pepper – deseeded and diced
225g/8oz tomatoes – diced
150ml/1/4pt vegetable stock

Sprinkle the aubergine with 2 teaspoonfuls of salt and leave to sit for 15 minutes. The salt will draw the bitterness and moisture out. Rinse thoroughly in a colander.

Heat the oil in a large pan and add the onions and garlic. Cook for a couple of minutes before adding the oregano and two-thirds of the parsley, the salt and pepper and tomato purée. Stir well, then add the pumpkin or squash, courgettes, red pepper, tomatoes, aubergines and stock. Mix well, bring to the boil, reduce the heat and cover. Simmer for 45–60 minutes, until all the vegetables are soft.

Serve hot, warm or cold, with the reserved parsley sprinkled over the top.

If you have never tried a butterflied leg of lamb on the barbecue, you are in for a treat. Ask your butcher to remove the bone, opening up the meat to create a butterfly shape. The lamb cooks much more quickly and is perfect for barbecuing or for flash roasting in a hot oven. This marinade adds delicious flavours and makes the meat irresistibly tender.

butterflied leg of lamb
with sweet ginger,
soy and spring onion glaze

serves 8–10

2.3kg/5lb leg of lamb – boned
3–4 dsp olive oil
2 dsp black peppercorns – lightly crushed

2–3 tbsp soy sauce
110g/4oz preserved stem ginger in syrup – finely sliced
3–4 spring onions – finely chopped

Using a sharp knife, score the lamb on the flesh side to open it up and flatten it as much as possible. The lamb should be almost rectangular.

In a large shallow dish, beat together the oil, peppercorns, soy sauce, ginger and spring onions. Place the lamb in the dish and coat it thoroughly with the marinade. Cover with cling film and refrigerate for 2–3 hours, turning from time to time. Remove the lamb from the dish and reserve the marinade.

Light the barbecue, heat a griddle pan or preheat the oven to 200°C/gas mark 6. Cook the lamb on the barbecue, on a griddle pan, or wrapped in foil in the oven for 25–30 minutes, depending on how pink you like your lamb. Baste during cooking with the marinade. Remove the lamb from the oven and allow it to rest for at least 10 minutes. Carve into thin slices and serve with pink potatoes.

pink potatoes

serves 4–5

450–700g/1–1 1/2lb baby new potatoes
2 dsp olive oil
2 tsp sun-dried tomato paste

4–5 sun-dried tomatoes – finely chopped
2 tbsp chopped fresh chives

Boil or steam the potatoes for 12–15 minutes, until they are cooked through. Drain then toss with the oil, sun-dried tomato paste and sun-dried tomatoes. Sprinkle with chives and serve hot.

This is a hearty and satisfying dinner. There are many variations of this dish and the leftovers can be used to make another traditional favourite, red flannel hash.

new england
boiled dinner

serves 8

1.8kg/4lb brisket or rump steak

curing spices

110–175g/4–6oz rock or sea salt
1 dsp paprika
2 tsp dried thyme
2 dsp black peppercorns – lightly crushed
2 bay leaves – chopped
1 tbsp ground allspice

accompaniments

700g/1 1/2 lb potatoes – cut into large chunks
225g/8oz small white boiling onions
225g/8oz turnips or swedes – cut into large chunks
450g/1lb carrots – cut into large chunks
225g/8oz parsnips – cut into large chunks
1/2 Savoy cabbage – outer leaves removed and
    cut into wedges

Pierce the meat all over with a skewer. For the curing, mix the salt, paprika, thyme, peppercorns, bay leaves and allspice in a large plastic bag. (The resealable type is ideal.) Place the meat in the bag and rub the spice mixture into it on all sides. Seal the bag, removing as much air as possible, place it in a shallow dish and and weigh it down. A scrubbed brick or a stone wrapped in foil or in a plastic bag is ideal. Chill in the fridge for 5–7 days, turning daily. This curing process extracts moisture from the meat and imparts a wonderful flavour.

Preheat the oven to 170°C/gas mark 3. Remove the beef from the bag and rinse it thoroughly with water. Place the meat in a large pan with sufficient water to cover by at least 2.5cm/1in. Bring to a gentle simmer and cook for 1 1/2–2 hours, skimming off any scum that comes to the surface. To test if the beef is cooked insert a skewer into the thickest part of the meat. If it slides out with ease, the beef is ready. Be careful not to cook the beef too fiercely or overcook it, as it will become tough.

Transfer the beef to an ovenproof dish. Pour over a ladleful of cooking liquid to keep the meat moist. Cover the dish tightly with foil and place in the oven to keep warm.

Add the root vegetables to the stock in the pot, bring to the boil, reduce the heat and part cover. Boil for 10–15 minutes. Add the cabbage and simmer for 8–10 minutes more, until all the vegetables are tender.

Slice the beef across the grain in thin slices. Drain the vegetables and arrange them around the beef. Moisten the meat with additional broth if necessary. Serve with horseradish soda bread (see page 106).

A very tasty way to use up any leftovers from the New England boiled dinner. Beetroots give the dish its distinctive red colour. It's delicious with a green salad, or with a poached egg on top.

red flannel
hash

serves 6

25g/1oz butter, or 2 tbsp olive oil
1 large onion – chopped
450g/1lb cooked beef – roughly chopped
4–5 cooked potatoes – roughly chopped
225g/8oz cooked beetroot – roughly chopped
450g/1lb cooked vegetables e.g turnips,
    carrots, parsnips

1 tbsp Worcestershire sauce
1 dsp hot chilli sauce
125ml/4floz cream
salt and freshly ground black pepper
chopped fresh parsley, to garnish

Preheat the oven to 200°C/gas mark 6.

Heat the butter or oil in a shallow heavy-based ovenproof pan. Add the onion and cook for 3–4 minutes, until the onion has softened. In a large bowl mix the beef, potatoes, beetroot, cooked vegetables, Worcestershire sauce, chilli sauce, cream and seasoning. Add to the onions in the pan, mix well, then press down firmly and even out the top to make a cake. After about 5–6 minutes, when the hash has started to set, transfer the pan to the oven and bake until the top is golden.

To serve, sprinkle the hash with parsley and cut into wedges.

I believe that there is nothing to match the flavour of a ham cooked on the bone. Ask your butcher how long you need to soak your ham for before cooking, or follow the instructions on the packaging, as the time varies according to the type of cure.

cider-baked
ham

serves 8–10

2.7–3.1kg/6–7lb ham – bone in, soaked,
　drained and rinsed thoroughly
1 onion
bouquet garni of 2–3 bay leaves, parsley stalks,
　thyme, 2–3 sage leaves and 1 celery stalk,
　tied together with string
8–10 cloves
570ml/1pt cider or unsweetened apple juice

glaze
125ml/4floz maple syrup
25g/1oz demerara sugar

Note the weight of the ham and then place it in a large saucepan with the onion, bouquet garni, cloves and cider or apple juice. Pour in enough water to cover. Bring to the boil, remove any scum and reduce the heat. Simmer gently for 1 hour. Allow the ham to cool slightly in the cooking liquid before removing it from the saucepan.

Preheat the oven to 180°C/gas mark 4. Place the ham on a piece of foil large enough to enclose it completely in a roasting tin. At this stage remove the skin, leaving the fat. Using a sharp knife, score the top of the ham diagonally, to form a diamond pattern. Sprinkle the syrup and sugar over the ham, and fold the edges of the foil together to enclose it completely.

Calculate the cooking time at about 40–60 minutes per kilo or 20–30 minutes per pound. Place in the oven. Thirty minutes before the end of the cooking time, increase the oven temperature to 200°C/gas mark 6 and open the foil to allow the ham to crisp. For a golden glaze, sprinkle a little extra maple syrup or demerara sugar over the ham for the final 10 minutes. Remove the ham from the oven and allow to stand for 15 minutes before carving.

oven-roasted squash

275g/10oz prepared butternut squash
  or pumpkin flesh – diced
2 red onions – cut into wedges
2.5–5cm/1–2in piece fresh root ginger –
  peeled and grated

1 tsp freshly grated nutmeg
25g/1oz butter
1 dsp olive oil
125ml/4floz maple syrup
125ml/4floz vegetable stock

Preheat the oven to 200°C/gas mark 6. Place the squash, onion, ginger, nutmeg, butter, oil and maple syrup in a large roasting dish. Mix well, pour over the stock and cook in the oven for 25–30 minutes, until the squash is tender. Serve hot.

McIntosh apples work very well in this sauce, but you can also try any of your favourite locally grown varieties of apple.

mcintosh apple sauce

4–6 McIntosh apples – peeled, cored and
  cut into wedges
1 dsp cider vinegar

50g/2oz soft brown sugar
2–3 tbsp water

Place the apples in a saucepan with the cider vinegar, sugar and water.
Stir well, then cook over a gentle heat, with the lid on, for 7–8 minutes or until the apples are frothy. Stir to reduce the apples to a smooth sauce. Serve hot.

Roasting the pumpkin with lemon-flavoured olive oil and garlic gives this risotto an irresistible flavour.

roasted pumpkin and
pancetta risotto

serves 4

450g/1lb prepared pumpkin flesh – cut into bite-sized chunks
6 dsp lemon-flavoured olive oil
5 garlic cloves – unpeeled
275ml/1/2pt dry white wine
1 red chilli – deseeded and finely chopped
3–4 spring onions – finely chopped

225g/8oz mushrooms – thickly sliced
225g/8oz risotto rice such as Arborio or Canaroli
275ml/1/2pt chicken or vegetable stock
110–175g/4–6oz pancetta – cut into chunks
2 dsp mascarpone cheese
50g/2oz Parmesan cheese shavings
1 dsp fresh flat-leaf parsley leaves

Preheat the oven to 200°C/gas mark 6. Place the pumpkin, three-quarters of the oil, the garlic and half the wine in a large ovenproof dish. Mix well, and roast in the oven for 30 minutes, or until the pumpkin is golden and soft.

In a large shallow pan, heat the remaining oil and gently fry the chilli, onions and mushrooms until the onions begin to soften, but not brown. If the mushrooms absorb too much oil, then add a little more. Add the rice and stir until all the grains are coated with oil and look shiny and translucent. Add the remaining wine and the stock. Stir well, ensuring that the rice is not stuck to the bottom of the pan. Simmer gently for 12–15 minutes, stirring occasionally, until the liquid has been absorbed.

Meanwhile, cook the pancetta in a hot frying pan for around 2–3 minutes until it is cooked through and crisp.

When the risotto is almost ready, squeeze the roasted garlic from its skin and add to the risotto. Stir in the mascarpone cheese and allow it to melt into the risotto. Spoon in the pumpkin and pancetta and mix very gently. Remove from the heat and scatter the Parmesan and parsley leaves over the top. Serve hot.

The risotto can be served in a pumpkin. Take one large pumpkin, cut off the top and remove most of the flesh. Brush the inside with oil and bake for 10 minutes. This will make the perfect serving dish for the risotto.

hickory-smoked
ribs

4 dsp olive oil
2–3 garlic cloves – finely chopped
1 onion – finely chopped
1 yellow pepper – deseeded and finely chopped
400g/14oz-can chopped tomatoes
4 dsp white wine vinegar
1 tsp English mustard

75g/3oz soft brown sugar
1 dsp soy sauce
125ml/4floz light beer, such as lager
125ml/4floz orange juice
salt and freshly ground black pepper
900g/2lb meaty pork spare ribs

Heat the oil in a saucepan and add the garlic, onion and yellow pepper. Cook gently for 3–4 minutes. Add the tomatoes, white wine vinegar, mustard, sugar, soy sauce, beer, orange juice and seasoning. Bring to the boil, reduce the heat and simmer gently for 10–12 minutes. The sauce will darken, thicken and lose its strong vinegar flavour. Leave to cool completely.

Place the spare ribs in a dish, pour over the sauce and turn the ribs to coat them evenly. Leave to marinate in the fridge for up to 24 hours.

Drain the excess sauce from the ribs and set it to one side. Light the barbecue, with soaked hickory wood chips on the coals, and cook the ribs when it is very hot. Cook, turning occasionally, until browned and tender. Brush the extra sauce over the ribs as they cook.

Alternatively, preheat the oven to 200°C/gas mark 6 and roast the ribs for 30–35 minutes, turning once or twice and brushing with the reserved marinade. Serve hot with a crisp green salad.

This is a simple dish in which the pork is cooked with maple syrup and herbs, and topped with potato and Parmesan. Easy, wholesome family fare.

homecoming
maple pork stew

serves 6–8

1 tbsp olive oil
small knob of butter for cooking
700–900g/1^1/2–2lb pork chops or medallions
1 onion – sliced into thick rings
1 red onion – sliced into thick rings
2 celery stalks – washed and cut into chunks
2 garlic cloves – chopped finely
1 tsp Dijon mustard
^{1}/2 tsp paprika

150ml/^{1}/4pt maple syrup
275ml/^{1}/2pt vegetable stock
2 tbsp chopped fresh tarragon
1 tbsp chopped fresh thyme
3–4 potatoes (about 900g/2lb) – cut into thick slices
25g/1oz butter
50g/2oz Parmesan cheese shavings
1 egg yolk – beaten (optional)

Preheat the oven to 180°C/gas mark 4. Heat the oil and butter in a large frying pan. Add the pork and brown the pieces over a high heat on both sides. Add the onions and continue cooking for 3–4 minutes. Next add the celery, garlic, mustard and paprika and continue cooking for a further 3–4 minutes.

Pour in the maple syrup and stir well to give everything in the pan a good coating of syrup. Pour in the stock and bring to the boil. Cook for a couple more minutes. Sprinkle a pinch each of the tarragon and thyme over the pork, and transfer to the casserole dish.

Place the potatoes in a saucepan. Cover with water and bring to the boil. Reduce the heat and cook for 3–5 minutes. Drain and return to the pan. Add the butter and half of the Parmesan cheese. Sprinkle in a pinch each of the tarragon and thyme. Turn the potatoes to coat the slices, and then spoon them over the top of the pork. For a golden glaze, brush with a little beaten egg yolk.

Bake for 1^1/2 hours with the lid on. Remove the lid 15 minutes before serving, and sprinkle with a little more of the thyme and tarragon, and the remainder of the cheese. Increase the oven temperature to 200°C/gas mark 6 for these final 15 minutes, to brown the cheese. Serve hot, garnished with the remaining herbs.

This cranberry and port sauce is great for serving with duck, but also works well with chicken and pork.

pan-fried duck breast
with port and cranberry sauce

serves 2

2 duck breasts
sea salt and freshly ground
    black pepper
1 dsp olive oil
25g/1oz butter

sauce
110g/4oz fresh cranberries
50g/2oz dried cranberries
150ml/¼pt port

2 dsp raspberry vinegar
50g/2oz butter
1 tsp wholegrain mustard
3 spring onions – cut into
    2.5cm/1in pieces
2–3 dsp redcurrant jelly

garnish
1 spring onion – cut into fine strips

Score the skin side of the duck breasts, and season well on the skin side with sea salt and pepper. Leave to one side for a moment or two.

In a bowl, mix the cranberries, port and raspberry vinegar for the sauce. Set aside while you cook the duck.

Heat the oil and butter in a frying pan. Add the duck breasts, skin sides down. Cook for 4–5 minutes until the skin is crisp and brown. Turn and cook the other side for 4–5 minutes. Remove the duck from the pan.

Pour away all but a dessertspoonful of the fat, and return the pan to the heat. Add the butter for the sauce, the mustard, spring onions and reserved cranberry mixture. Bring to the boil, reduce the heat and cook for 5–6 minutes, until some of the cranberries have popped and softened a little.

Add the redcurrant jelly and stir until it has melted. Return the duck breasts and any juices to the pan and reheat gently for 2–3 minutes.

Garnish with spring onions and serve immediately.

A light apple sauce with a twist – perfect for enlivening simply cooked pork or duck.

apple-cider
sauce

serves 4

1 Bramley apple – peeled, cored and finely sliced
1 garlic clove – finely chopped
pinch of soft brown sugar
1 tbsp cider vinegar

1 small onion – minced or finely chopped
1 tsp chopped fresh thyme
1/2 tsp freshly ground black pepper
1 dsp maple syrup

Heat the apples in a saucepan with the garlic, sugar and cider vinegar, stirring until the sugar has dissolved. Cover and cook for about 5 minutes, until the apple is softened. Add the onion, thyme, black pepper and maple syrup. Cook slowly over a low heat, stirring occasionally, for 8–10 minutes. Serve hot.

Preserve the best of the apple crop (any kind) at season's end, so that you have delicious chutney to enjoy throughout the year.

season-end apple
chutney

makes 1.8kg/4lb

450g/1lb apples – peeled, cored and diced
450g/1lb tomatoes – chopped
450g/1lb onions – chopped
450g/1lb sultanas
2 garlic cloves – chopped

2 tbsp ground ginger
1/2 tsp ground mace
1/2 tsp ground allspice
570ml/1pt white vinegar
450g/1lb soft brown sugar

Preheat the oven to 190°C/gas mark 5.

Place the apples, tomatoes, onions, sultanas, garlic, ginger, mace, allspice and vinegar in a large preserving pan. Mix well and bring to the boil, uncovered. Simmer for 30 minutes. Meanwhile, spread the sugar on a baking tray and place in the oven for 10–12 minutes. Allow the contents of the preserving pan to cool a little before adding the warmed sugar. Stir until dissolved. Carefully pour the hot chutney into warmed sterilised jars (see page 123) and immediately cover with waxed discs and airtight lids.

Pot-roasting is a way of cooking that most of us have forgotten about. Yet it is a wonderfully simple method that brings out the best flavour in the meat.

pot-roast
chicken
with sage and cider

serves 6

1 chicken (weighing 1.3–1.8kg/3–4lb)
2 tsp English mustard
4–6 sage leaves – finely chopped
2–3 dsp olive oil
2 red onions – cut into chunks
2 onions – cut into chunks
4 celery stalks – cut into 5cm/2in pieces

275ml/^{1}/2pt chicken or vegetable stock
275ml/^{1}/2pt cider
2 red apples – cored and cut into wedges
2 green apples – cored and cut into wedges
8–10 small potatoes – halved
275ml/^{1}/2pt cream
salt and freshly ground black pepper

Preheat the oven to 200°C/gas mark 6.

Pat the chicken dry using kitchen paper. Spread the mustard on the breast and legs and sprinkle with sage. Heat the oil in a large heavy-based casserole dish and brown the chicken well on all sides for 8–10 minutes. Remove the chicken.

Add the onions and celery and cook for 4–5 minutes. Return the chicken to the dish, breast-side up, and add the stock and cider. Cover, bring to the boil, turn down the heat and simmer for 5–6 minutes.

Transfer to the oven and cook for 30 minutes. Add the apples, potatoes, cream and seasoning, reduce the oven temperature to 170°C/gas mark 3 and cook for a further 25–30 minutes until the chicken is cooked through and the potatoes are tender. Serve hot with plenty of the delicious cooking juices.

thanksgiving and christmas

Harvest-time in the pumpkin fields in North Andover

Roast turkey forms the central part of the celebratory Thanksgiving meal.
Try to buy a free-range organic bird – the flavour will be wonderful.

thanksgiving
turkey

serves 10–12

4–5kg/10–12lb turkey
1 onion
1 carrot
1 celery stalk – broken in half
3–4 bay leaves – creased in half

1–2 sprigs of sage
110–175g/4–6oz butter – softened
salt and freshly ground black pepper
10–12 rindless rashers streaky bacon
4 dsp redcurrant jelly – warmed

Preheat the oven to 200°C/gas mark 6. Remove the giblets and pat the turkey
dry, inside and out, using kitchen paper. This will ensure a lovely crisp skin.

Place the onion, carrot, celery, bay leaves and sage inside the turkey. These
ingredients will impart moisture and flavour during roasting. It is important that
you leave plenty of space inside the bird for the air to circulate when cooking,
to ensure that the inside reaches the required temperature to cook through.

If you are using stuffing (see page 73), put it into the neck end of the turkey,
under the flap of skin.

Line a roasting dish with a double layer of foil, large enough to completely
enclose the turkey. Lift the turkey in. Spread butter all over it and cover with
bacon in a lattice pattern. Fold the foil around the turkey so that it is completely
enclosed.

Roast the turkey for 45 minutes. Then reduce the temperature to 170°C/gas
mark 3 and cook for a further 3^1/2 hours. Baste every 30–40 minutes during
cooking to keep the turkey moist. Take care to avoid splitting the foil, and
re-close it carefully during this process.

About 30 minutes before the end of the cooking time, remove the turkey from
the oven and open the foil. Remove the bacon, baste, and then spoon over the
redcurrant jelly. Increase the temperature to 200°C/gas mark 6 for the final 30
minutes to brown and crisp the skin.

To check if the turkey is cooked, pierce the thickest part of the thigh with a
skewer. If the juices run clear then the turkey is ready. Pink juices mean that the
meat is still slightly undercooked – continue cooking and test again. Allow to
relax for 20–25 minutes before carving. This will ensure that the turkey is moist.
Use the juices remaining in the roasting dish to make gravy (see page 72).

It's usual to serve gravy, a variety of sauces and often a choice of stuffings with Thanksgiving dinner. Try some of these accompaniments with your Thanksgiving or Christmas turkey.

traditional
gravy

serves 6–8

Well-flavoured gravy is part of the success of any roast meal. Use a sturdy, thick-based roasting tin to cook your joint of meat or poultry. When you have removed the cooked meat from the roasting tin, skim off any excess fat, leaving behind the flavoursome juices. Rest the meat while you make the gravy.

Place the roasting tin over a low heat. Sprinkle in a little plain flour and stir into the juices until it forms a smooth paste. Add some hot water or stock, until you have the desired consistency, and bring to the boil, stirring well. Simmer for around 1 minute, season, and serve. As an approximate guide, 25g/1oz flour to 275ml/1/2pt liquid will make a thicker gravy; 25g/1oz flour to 570ml/1pt liquid will make a thinner gravy.

variations

Stir in around 1 dsp redcurrant jelly just before serving for a wonderful colour and flavour.

Add around 1 dsp cranberry jelly or sauce for a delicious Christmas or Thanksgiving gravy.

Add 1/2 tsp mustard for an added kick.

Try a dash of Worcestershire sauce.

Replacing some of the stock with red or white wine adds wonderful depth of flavour. Red wine goes best with gravy for beef or lamb, and white wine works beautifully with turkey and chicken.

cornmeal **stuffing**

serves 10–12

175g/6oz cornmeal or polenta
275ml/½pt chicken stock
50g/2oz butter
salt and freshly ground black pepper
2 dsp olive oil
1 onion – finely chopped
2 celery stalks – diced

½ tsp celery salt
2 tsp finely chopped fresh thyme
2 tsp finely chopped fresh sage
110g/4oz white or wholemeal
   breadcrumbs
1 egg – lightly beaten

In a large saucepan, heat together the cornmeal or polenta, stock, half of the butter and seasoning until the cornmeal has absorbed the stock. Stir continuously until the mixture leaves the sides of the pan. This will take about 1 minute. Spread the mixture on a baking sheet and leave to cool and dry out a little.

In a frying pan, heat the remaining butter with the olive oil. Add the onion, celery, celery salt, thyme and sage. Allow to cook for a minute or two, and then add the breadcrumbs. Remove from the heat, add the cornmeal and egg, and mix well.

Use the stuffing to stuff the neck flap of the turkey. Loosen the skin around the neck with your fingers, then pack the stuffing in. Remember to weigh the stuffed bird when calculating the cooking time. Alternatively bake the stuffing for 30–35 minutes in a covered casserole or ovenproof dish in an oven preheated to 180°C/gas mark 4.

spiced cranberry and **apple stuffing**

serves 6–8

225g/8oz cranberries
25g/1oz soft brown sugar
110g/4oz white breadcrumbs
1 large onion – finely chopped
¼ tsp ground cloves

½ tsp ground mace
¼ tsp ground cinnamon
3 Bramley apples – unpeeled,
   cored and diced
50g/2oz butter – melted

Toss the cranberries with the sugar in a large bowl. Add the breadcrumbs, onion, cloves, mace, cinnamon and apples and mix thoroughly. Pour over the butter and mix again.

Stuff the turkey in the way described above. Alternatively bake the stuffing for 25–30 minutes in a covered casserole or ovenproof dish in an oven preheated to 180°C/gas mark 4.

Here is a very simple cranberry sauce that brings out the best in the flavour and appearance of this wonderful bouncing berry.

confit of cranberries

serves 4–6

450g/1lb cranberries
110g/4oz soft brown sugar
275ml/1/2pt red wine

4 tbsp raspberry vinegar
grated zest and juice of 1/2 orange

Place all the ingredients in a small saucepan and heat gently until the sugar has dissolved. Then bring just to the boil, immediately reduce the heat and simmer for 15–20 minutes but do not allow the berries to break down as this will spoil their appearance. Serve hot or cold.

A slightly livelier version of a traditional cranberry sauce. It's ready in minutes and packed with flavour.

cranberry sauce
with a hint of heat

serves 4–6

225g/8oz fresh cranberries
1 McIntosh apple – peeled, cored and cut
    into chunks
2 tbsp olive oil
1 small onion – finely chopped

1/2 red pepper – deseeded and chopped
1/2 tsp chilli sauce
1 tbsp honey
150ml/1/4pt apple juice
salt and freshly ground black pepper

Coarsely purée the cranberries and apple in a blender without allowing them to become too smooth – they should retain some texture.

Heat the oil in a pan, add the onion and red pepper, and cook gently for 2–3 minutes. Add the puréed cranberries and apple, chilli sauce, honey and apple juice. Simmer gently for 4–5 minutes, then season to taste. Serve hot.

This easy fresh chutney is delicious served with cold meats, especially turkey, and cheeses. It will keep for a couple of weeks in well-sealed, sterilised containers (see page 123) in the fridge.

no-cook clementine and
cranberry chutney

makes 700g/1½lb

225g/8oz soft brown sugar
450g/1lb cranberries
4–6 clementines – peeled or unpeeled,
   coarsely chopped

2 dsp redcurrant jelly or pecan
   pepper jelly
1 tsp chopped fresh mint

Preheat the oven to 190°C/gas mark 5. Spread the sugar on a baking tray and place in the oven for 10–12 minutes.

In a blender, whizz the cranberries and clementines until well mixed. The fruit should be chunky not smooth. Transfer to a bowl and stir in the jelly and sugar. Mix well, then cover with cling film and leave to sit at room temperature, stirring occasionally, until all the sugar has dissolved. Chill, and scatter with mint before serving.

Corn was a staple crop of the early American settlers and has always graced harvest and Thanksgiving tables. If you are looking for a new vegetable idea, this delicious dish is perfect for you.

fresh fall
succotash

4 large cobs of sweetcorn
50g/2oz butter
1 small red onion – finely chopped
1/2 red pepper – deseeded and chopped
450g/1lb green beans – cut into 2.5cm/1in
    long pieces
125ml/4floz chicken or vegetable stock
salt and freshly ground black pepper

curry butter
25g/1oz butter – softened
1 tsp mild curry powder

Boil the sweetcorn in salted water for 4–5 minutes, or until the kernels begin to soften. Allow the corn to cool slightly, then remove the kernels by cutting down the cobs with a sharp knife.

Melt the butter in a large pan. Add the onion and red pepper and cook for 3–4 minutes, or until the onion is softened. Add the green beans, sweetcorn, stock and seasoning. Bring to the boil, reduce the heat and simmer gently for 4–5 minutes, or until all the vegetables are tender.

Mix the butter and curry powder together. Serve the hot succotash with the curry butter melting over the top.

These potatoes have a wonderful texture – somewhere between mash and roast potatoes.

crushed potatoes
with parmesan

1–1.3kg/2 ½–3lb potatoes – cut into chunks
1 dsp olive oil
25g/1oz butter
salt and freshly ground black pepper

1 dsp coarsely chopped fresh herbs
  (e.g. mint, parsley, chives)
110g/4oz Parmesan shavings

Preheat the oven to 200°C/gas mark 6.

Place the potatoes in a saucepan and boil for 10–15 minutes until just showing signs of softening. Meanwhile, place the oil and butter in a roasting tin and heat in the oven until the butter has melted and the oil is hot (around 5 minutes). Drain the potatoes and toss in the roasting tin until they are well coated.

Roast for 8–10 minutes until the potatoes are cooked through and beginning to become crisp. Remove from the oven and, using a fork or masher, coarsely break them up. Season well, garnish with herbs and sprinkle with Parmesan. Mix well and serve immediately.

This Christmas pudding is given a fabulous American flavour with cranberries, blueberries, pecan nuts, maple syrup and bourbon. If you want to make the pudding well in advance, use dried fruit instead of fresh. Remember to make a wish while mixing the pudding!

irish-american
christmas pudding

serves 8–10

110g/4oz fresh cranberries
225g/8oz dried cranberries
110g/4oz fresh or dried blueberries
110g/4oz pecan nuts – roughly chopped
225g/8oz sultanas
110g/4oz glacé cherries – chopped
grated zest and juice of 1 orange
1 apple – peeled and grated
2 dsp maple syrup
1/2 tsp freshly grated nutmeg

1/2 tsp ground cloves
1/2 tsp ground cinnamon
6 tbsp bourbon
225g/8oz butter
225g/8oz soft brown sugar
3 eggs – lightly beaten
110g/4oz plain flour – sifted
110g/4oz white or brown breadcrumbs
1–2 tbsp bourbon, to flame

Place the cranberries in a small saucepan and cook over a very low heat for a few minutes, just until they have softened a little. Pour the cooked cranberries and any juice into a large bowl. Add the dried cranberries, blueberries, pecan nuts, sultanas, cherries, orange zest and orange juice, apple, maple syrup, spices and bourbon. Cover with cling film and leave for 24 hours to allow the fruits to absorb the liquid and plump up.

Cream the butter and sugar until light and fluffy. Add a little beaten egg, a little flour and some of the breadcrumbs and mix. Do not add all the egg without the flour and breadcrumbs as this will cause the mixture to curdle. Repeat until the egg, flour and breadcrumbs are used up. Mix in the steeped fruits until thoroughly combined.

Grease two 900g/2lb pudding basins. Divide the mixture between the basins. Cover with a secure lid or a double layer of well-greased greaseproof paper, making a fold in the paper to allow for expansion during cooking. Top with folded foil. Tie securely with string or use an elastic band, and boil or steam for 3 1/2–4 hours.

Store the puddings for 1–2 weeks to allow the flavours to develop. Boil or steam for 1 hour before serving. Turn out onto a large plate. Heat the bourbon in a small pan for a few seconds. Pour it over the hot pudding and immediately set it alight. If the pudding has cooled slightly, light the bourbon in the pan and then pour it over. Serve immediately with warm egg-nog sauce (see page 81).

A great favourite for Thanksgiving in America, this is one of those recipes you will love, and turn to time and time again. The secret lies in using a good mature Irish cheddar cheese paired with local apples – my favourites are Bramleys from County Armagh.

cheddar crust
apple pie

serves 8–10

4 large bramley apples – peeled, cored and
   finely sliced
grated zest and juice of 1 lemon
50g/2oz caster sugar
50g/2oz plain flour
1/2 tsp ground cinnamon
50g/2oz butter

pastry
225g/8oz plain flour
pinch of salt
125g/4 1/2oz butter – softened
50g/2oz mature cheddar cheese – coarsely grated
1 egg yolk
1–2 tbsp water

glaze
25g/1oz mature cheddar cheese – coarsely grated
1 egg – beaten (to glaze)

To make the pastry, place the flour, salt and butter in a food processor. Whizz until reduced to crumbs, then add the cheese, egg yolk and sufficient water to bind the pastry and whizz again. Wrap in cling film and leave to relax in the fridge for at least 15 minutes before rolling out.

Preheat the oven to 190°C/gas mark 5.

In a large bowl, mix the apples, lemon zest and juice, sugar, flour and cinnamon.

Halve the pastry and roll out one piece to line a deep pie plate measuring about 18cm/7in in diameter. Pile the apples on top of the pastry and dot with butter. Brush the rim of the pastry with some cold water. Roll out the remaining pastry into a circle large enough to cover the apples. Press the pastry edges together to seal. Trim off any excess overhanging the plate. Decorate with leaves made from any trimmings and make a small hole in the centre of the pie.

Bake for approximately 20 minutes, until the the pastry is beginning to firm up. Brush with the egg and sprinkle with the cheddar cheese to glaze. Cook for a further 10 minutes, until the pastry is golden brown and the pie is cooked through. Serve warm.

warm egg-nog
sauce

serves 8–10

570ml/1pt whipping cream –
  lightly whisked
250ml/8floz milk
5 eggs
200g/7oz caster sugar

1/2 tsp natural vanilla extract
1/2 tsp freshly grated nutmeg
180ml/6floz brandy
60ml/21/2floz dark rum

Heat the cream and milk to just below boiling point. Remove from the heat. In a large bowl, whisk the eggs for 2–3 minutes, until very frothy. Gradually whisk in the sugar. Place the bowl over a pan of barely simmering water and heat gently, stirring all the time with the whisk. Pour in the hot milk and cream. Add the vanilla, half the nutmeg, the brandy and rum. Continue to stir until the mixture has thickened and lost its eggy flavour. Do not allow the mixture to get too hot or it will curdle. Sprinkle with the remaining nutmeg and serve with the Irish-American Christmas pudding on page 78.

rum and pecan
sauce

serves 4

75g/3oz soft brown sugar
275ml/1/2pt water
75g/3oz butter
4 dsp dark rum

1 dsp maple syrup
25g/1oz cornflour, mixed to a paste
  with a little cold water
75g/3oz pecan nuts – roughly chopped

Place all the ingredients except the pecan nuts in a saucepan and bring to the boil, stirring. Reduce the heat, add the pecan nuts and simmer for 1 minute. Serve with pumpkin pie (see page 82).

I'm sure that you've all heard the expression 'as American as apple pie'. This is another delicious pie that is even more American. Don't worry if you want to make this when fresh pumpkin is not in season – canned purée works very well in this recipe.

pumpkin
pie

serves 8–10

pastry
225g/8oz plain flour
150g/5oz butter – softened
25g/1oz icing sugar
1 egg

filling
450g/1lb prepared fresh pumpkin flesh – cut into chunks, or canned pumpkin purée

275ml/¹/2pt double cream
50g/2oz butter – softened
50g/2oz soft brown sugar
2 eggs – lightly beaten
1 tsp ground cinnamon
1 tsp ground ginger
1 tsp freshly grated nutmeg
1 tsp ground allspice
1 tsp natural vanilla extract

Preheat the oven to 200°C/gas mark 6. Place the fresh pumpkin (if using) in an ovenproof dish and bake for 30–45 minutes, until soft and cooked through. Whizz in a blender until very smooth.

Place the flour, butter, icing sugar and egg in a food processor, and whizz until the mixture comes together. Turn out onto a floured surface and roll out, then use to line a flan tin measuring approximately 23cm/9in in diameter. Trim excess pastry from around the edge using a knife and reserve the trimmings.

Roll out the trimmings and use them to cut out leaf shapes (or other shapes). Brush the edge of the pastry with water and stick the leaves on to form a border the whole way around the edge of the tin. As well as looking decorative, these will provide a little extra height and help to stop the filling from leaking during cooking. Cover the pastry case with clingfilm and chill while you prepare the filling.

In a large bowl mix the pumpkin purée and cream. In a separate large bowl, cream the butter and sugar until light and fluffy, then beat in the eggs a little at a time. Add the cinnamon, ginger, nutmeg, allspice, vanilla extract and pumpkin mixture, stirring continuously to ensure the mixture is smooth.

Pour the filling into the pastry case until it reaches the edge of the pastry shapes. Bake for 35–45 minutes, until the filling is set and lightly browned. If you are unable to get all the filling in at first, add a little more after the pie has been in the oven for about 15 minutes, when the filling has already started to set.

Serve warm, with rum and pecan sauce (see page 81).

desserts

Visiting the heritage orchard at Smolak's farm in North Andover

This cheesecake is light, zesty and refreshing, and even more delicious with the topping of boozy blueberries.

baked lemon and vanilla
cheesecake
with boozy blueberries

serves 8

175g/6oz almond biscuits
50g/2oz butter
1 dsp maple syrup
565g/1¼lb cream cheese
110g/4oz caster sugar
grated zest of 2 lemons
1 tsp natural vanilla extract
6 eggs – well beaten
125ml/4floz sour cream or natural yoghurt

boozy blueberries
450g/1lb blueberries
25g/1oz arrowroot
2 dsp water
4 dsp Irish Mist, or other liqueur

Preheat the oven to 140°C/gas mark 1. Line and lightly grease a 23cm/9in springform tin.

Place the almond biscuits in a plastic bag and crush with a rolling pin to fine crumbs. Melt the butter in a saucepan, add the biscuits and maple syrup and stir until well mixed. Then press firmly into the base of the prepared tin.

Cream the cheese with the sugar, lemon zest and vanilla extract in a large bowl. Then add the eggs, a little at a time, mixing continuously. Finally, stir in the sour cream or yoghurt until smooth. Spread the topping over the base and bake for 1–1¼ hours, until just firm and lightly golden on top. Allow to cool.

To make the boozy blueberries, place the blueberries in a large saucepan. In a small bowl mix the arrowroot and water to a smooth paste. Add this to the blueberries. Bring to the boil, simmer gently for no more than 1 minute then add the Irish Mist. Allow to cool, then spoon over the top of the cheesecake.

This is one of those moreish tarts – you just won't be able to help going back for another slice. If you like a more intense flavour, try roasting the nuts on a baking sheet in an oven preheated to 200°C/gas mark 6 for 10–12 minutes before you start.

toffee and nut
tart

pastry
225g/8oz plain flour
25g/1oz caster sugar
75g/3oz butter
1 tsp natural vanilla extract
2–3 dsp milk

filling
75g/3oz soft brown sugar
4 dsp maple syrup or honey
75g/3oz butter

75ml/3floz double cream
2 tbsp bourbon
110g/4oz walnuts
75g/3oz hazelnuts
75g/3oz pecan nuts
50g/2oz ground almonds
¼ tsp ground cinnamon

decoration
25g/1oz icing sugar
¼ tsp ground cinnamon

Preheat the oven to 200°C/gas mark 6.

Place the flour, sugar, butter, vanilla extract and milk in a food processor and whizz until the ingredients begin to bind together. Add a little more milk if necessary, to help the mixture to bind. Turn out onto a lightly floured surface, knead lightly and roll out, and use to line a 20–23cm/8–9in tart tin. Chill for around 15 minutes before blind baking (see page 122) for 10–15 minutes. Set aside to cool while you make the filling.

Reduce the oven temperature to 180°C/gas mark 4.

To make the filling, heat the brown sugar, maple sugar or honey and butter in a saucepan. Bring to the boil, turn down the heat and simmer for 4–5 minutes until caramelised. Cool slightly. Add the cream, bourbon, walnuts, hazelnuts, pecan nuts, ground almonds and cinnamon and mix well. Pour this mixture over the pastry base and bake for around 15 minutes until the filling has set. Cool slightly and dust with icing sugar and a little cinnamon. Serve warm or cold, with cream or yoghurt.

This is an old-fashioned New England dessert of apples topped with maple-flavoured sponge. Maple sugar is made from the sap of the maple tree, but if you can't track it down, use caster sugar instead. Make sure that the butter you use is very soft so that it folds easily into the mixture.

apple-maple
pandowdy

700g/1 1/2lbs Bramley apples – peeled, cored and cut into wedges
1 tsp ground cinnamon
2 tbsp maple sugar or caster sugar
4 tbsp maple syrup

topping
110g/4oz plain flour
1/2 tsp ground cinnamon
1/2 tsp freshly grated nutmeg
2 tsp baking powder

50g/2oz caster sugar
1 egg – lightly beaten
75ml/3floz milk
1 tsp natural vanilla extract
1 dsp maple syrup
75g/3oz butter – softened

to serve
25g/1oz icing sugar

Preheat the oven to 180°C/gas mark 4. Butter an ovenproof dish, such as a deep pie dish. Place the apples in the dish and add the cinnamon and maple sugar or caster sugar. Pour over the maple syrup, cover with foil and bake for 20–25 minutes, until the apples have softened slightly.

Sift the flour, cinnamon, nutmeg and baking powder into a bowl, then add the sugar. In another bowl, beat the egg with the milk and vanilla extract. Slowly add this to the flour mixture, stirring all the time, but being careful not to overbeat. Add the maple syrup and keep stirring to form a batter-like mixture. Fold in the butter.

Pour the batter over the apples, ensuring it covers them completely, and return the dish to the oven. Cook, uncovered, for 20–25 minutes, until the topping is golden and firm. Dust with icing sugar and serve warm, with whipped cream or yoghurt.

A perfect dessert for autumn, when our Irish pears are at their very best.

walnut-crusted
poached pears
with orange-scented mascarpone

4 pears – cored from the base
$^1/_2$ tsp ground cinnamon
4 dsp demerara sugar
50g/2oz walnuts – finely chopped
150ml/$^1/_4$pt maple syrup
150ml/$^1/_4$pt freshly squeezed orange juice
grated zest of $^1/_2$ orange
1 vanilla pod
4 cinnamon sticks

orange-scented mascarpone
110g/4oz mascarpone cheese
1 dsp maple syrup
grated zest of $^1/_2$ orange

Preheat the oven to 180°C/gas mark 4.

Stand the pears in an ovenproof dish, which holds them neatly. In a bowl, mix together the cinnamon, demerara sugar and walnuts. Fill the cavities in the pears with this mixture and sprinkle the remainder around the fruit in the dish.

Mix the maple syrup, orange juice and orange zest. Split open the vanilla pod and add it to the liquid mixture. Pour over the pears. Push a cinnamon stick into the top of each pear to resemble a stalk and bake for 12–15 minutes, until the pears are crusted and soft. Leave to cool a little while you make the orange-scented mascarpone.

Mix the mascarpone, maple syrup and orange zest. Serve with the warm pears.

Sheer decadence: an irresistible pie with the American flavours of cranberry, pecan and maple syrup.

cranberry, pear and
pecan pie
with honeyed mascarpone

serves 6–8

175g/6oz plain flour – sifted
25g/1oz caster sugar
75g/3oz ground almonds
110g/4oz butter – softened
1 egg – lightly beaten

filling
175g/6oz cranberries
4 pears – peeled, cored and diced
25g/1oz caster sugar
3 large eggs

75g/3oz soft brown sugar
25g/1oz butter – melted
5 tbsp maple syrup or honey
110g/4oz pecan nuts
grated zest and juice of 1 lemon

honeyed mascarpone
200g/7oz mascarpone cheese
4 dsp low-fat natural yoghurt
1 tbsp honey

Place the flour in the food processor, then add the sugar, ground almonds, butter and egg. Blend until the mixture binds together – add a little water if necessary – then transfer to a floured surface. Roll out gently (this is a very short pastry) and use to line a loose-bottomed flan tin, 18–20 cm/7–8 in in diameter. To transfer the pastry easily to the dish, slide the loose bottom under the pastry and then just drop it into the tin.

Wrap the lined flan tin in clingfilm and chill for 15–20 minutes. Preheat the oven to 180°C/gas mark 4. Blind bake the pastry case (see page 122) for 12–15 minutes.

Turn the oven down to 170°C/gas mark 3. Place the cranberries, pears and caster sugar in a bowl and mix.

Beat the eggs with the brown sugar until light and creamy. Add the melted butter and maple syrup, and beat again. Add the sugar-coated berries and pears, most of the nuts (keep a few for the top), and the lemon zest and juice. Mix gently, then spoon into the pastry case. Arrange the reserved nuts on top. Bake for 25–30 minutes, until the pastry is cooked through and the filling has set.

To make the honeyed mascarpone, mix the mascarpone with the yoghurt and honey. Allow the pie to cool slightly before serving with the mascarpone.

These brownies are a real treat and have a wonderfully sticky texture. Serve them with balsamic ice cream (see page 94) for a mouthwateringly good dessert.

hazelnut and cappuccino
brownies

makes 9

110g/4oz butter
150g/5oz chocolate – milk or dark,
    broken into pieces
2 dsp strong black coffee (Camp or instant)
1 dsp maple syrup
2 eggs
350g/12oz soft brown sugar
50g/2oz plain flour
1 tsp ground cinnamon
50g/2oz hazelnuts – roughly chopped

topping
110g/4oz chocolate
75g/3oz butter
1 tsp strong black coffee (Camp or instant)
1/2 tsp ground cinnamon

Preheat the oven to 180°C/gas mark 4. Line and grease a 20cm/8in square tin.

Melt the butter and and chocolate together in a saucepan, over a low heat. Mix the coffee with the maple syrup and add this to the chocolate. Remove from the heat and cool a little.

Whisk the eggs with 1 dessertspoon of the sugar in a large bowl until light and fluffy. Add the rest of the sugar and whisk until thick and creamy. Fold in the cooled chocolate and butter mixture. Sift in the flour, and add the cinnamon and hazelnuts. Stir well.

Pour the mixture into the prepared tin and bake for 30–35 minutes, until risen, set and slightly springy to the touch. Allow to cool in the tin.

To make the topping, melt the chocolate and butter in a bowl over a pan of simmering water. Add the coffee and cinnamon and mix well until combined. Cool and chill for about 10 minutes until the topping thickens and then spread on top of the brownies. Leave to set. Cut into nine squares and serve.

Although balsamic vinegar might seem an unusual ingredient for a dessert, it gives a wonderful rich colour and a delightful flavour to this ice cream. It's perfect with hazelnut cappuccino brownies (see page 92), or with strawberries.

balsamic
ice cream

serves 6

2 dsp water
275g/10oz caster sugar
4 dsp balsamic vinegar
5 egg yolks

570ml/1pt milk
150ml/¼pt double or whipping cream
½ tsp natural vanilla extract

To make the balsamic syrup, heat the water and 225g/8oz of the sugar gently in a saucepan, stirring until the sugar has dissolved completely. Bring to the boil and stop stirring, then boil for 5–6 minutes until the mixture caramelises, becoming a light golden brown colour. Dip the base of the pan into a bowl (or sink) of cold water to stop the caramel getting any darker. Leave to cool for about 5 minutes, then add the balsamic vinegar, stirring well.

To make a custard base for the ice cream, beat the egg yolks with the remaining sugar until light and creamy. In another saucepan, heat the milk and cream. Add the egg mixture and vanilla essence to the milk and cream and heat gently, but do not allow to boil. When the mixture shows signs of thickening, remove from the heat. Add the balsamic syrup and mix well.

freezing the ice cream
Either transfer the mixture to an ice cream machine and follow the instructions, or pour it into a shallow plastic container and place in the coolest part of your freezer for at least 2½–3 hours. After 1–1½ hours, place the partially frozen ice cream in a food processor and whizz until smooth before returning it to the freezer. Repeat this process a couple more times during freezing to ensure the ice cream is smooth.

pecan nut
ice cream

5 egg yolks – beaten
25g/1oz caster sugar
$^1/4$ tsp natural vanilla extract
125ml/4floz maple syrup

275ml/$^1/2$pt double cream
125ml/4floz milk
75g/3oz pecan nuts – half finely chopped and half coarsely chopped

Beat the egg yolks, sugar and vanilla in a bowl until light and creamy. In a saucepan, heat the maple syrup, cream and milk. Add a little of the warmed milk and cream to the egg mixture and mix well. Return this mixture to the remaining milk and cream in the pan and heat gently, stirring continuously, but do not allow to boil. When the mixture shows signs of thickening, remove from the heat. Stir in the pecan nuts.

Follow the instructions for freezing ice cream on the opposite page.

pistachio nut
ice cream

4 egg yolks
75g/3oz caster sugar
25g/1oz cornflour
275ml/$^1/2$pt milk
275ml/$^1/2$pt whipping or double cream

grated zest of 2 limes
juice of $^1/2$ lime
150g/5oz pistachio nuts – roughly chopped
few drops of green food colouring (optional)

Beat the egg yolks, sugar and cornflour in a bowl until light and creamy. In a saucepan, heat the milk. Add a little of the warmed milk to the egg mixture and mix well. Then return this mixture to the remaining milk and cream in the pan and heat gently, stirring continuously, but do not allow to boil. When the mixture shows signs of thickening, remove from the heat and leave to cool.

In a large bowl, whip the cream into soft peaks. Fold in the lime zest and juice, and 110g/4oz of the chopped pistachio nuts. Add a few drops of green colouring if you wish. Mix the cooled custard into the cream a little at a time.

Follow the instructions for freezing ice cream on the opposite page.

Serve the ice cream with the reserved chopped pistachio nuts sprinkled over the top.

There are many variations of this famous pie. The recipe below is my favourite.

key lime pie

275g/10oz plain flour – sifted
25g/1oz icing sugar – sifted
175g/6oz unsalted butter
1 egg yolk
1–2 dsp milk

filling
4 eggs
2 egg yolks
175g/6oz caster sugar
juice of 4 limes
grated zest of 2 limes
175g/6oz butter – softened
275ml/1/2pt double cream

Preheat the oven to 180°C/gas mark 4.

To make the pastry, place the flour, icing sugar, butter, egg yolk and milk in a food processor. Whizz until mixed. Add a little more milk if the mixture does not come together. Wrap the pastry in clingfilm and place in the fridge to relax for 20–25 minutes.

Roll out the pastry and line a 21–23cm (8–9inch) diameter flan tin or dish. Prick the base of the pastry all over with a fork to stop it rising and then blind bake (see page 122) for 12–15 minutes.

To make the filling, beat the eggs and egg yolks with the caster sugar in a large heatproof bowl. Place the bowl over a pan of gently simmering water (or pour the mixture into the top of a double saucepan) and stir until it is thick and creamy – this will take about 5 minutes.

Remove from the heat and add the lime juice and zest, stirring gently. Add the softened butter a little at a time and continue to stir. Finally, fold in the double cream until the mixture becomes smooth.

Pour the filling into the pastry case and bake for 25 minutes. Allow to cool.

I like to serve this with pistachio nut ice cream (see page 95).

A new twist on hot fruit salad, made here with berries and Irish liqueurs. You can use any assortment of your favourite berries, but try to keep the overall weight the same. This is particularly good served over pecan nut ice cream (see page 95).

irish-american
flambé

serves 4–6

25g/1oz butter
110g/4oz cranberries
225g/8oz strawberries
110g/4oz blackberries
225g/8oz blueberries
50g/2oz demerara sugar
4 tbsp Irish Mist liqueur

4 tbsp Irish cream liqueur
50g/2oz dried pears – sliced
50g/2oz whole pecan nuts or walnuts
$1/2$ tsp ground cinnamon
$1/2$ tsp freshly grated nutmeg
sprigs of fresh mint

Heat the butter in a saucepan or deep frying pan over a low heat. Add the cranberries and cook for a minute or so. Add the strawberries, blackberries and blueberries and sprinkle with the sugar. Cook gently for no longer than 1 minute.

Heat the Irish Mist in a small pan, then pour it over the berries and light it carefully. Once the flames have died down, add the Irish cream liqueur, dried pears, nuts, cinnamon and nutmeg. Stir gently until the fruit and nuts are combined, and turn off the heat. Be careful not to overcook as this will spoil the fruit.

Serve warm, spooned over pecan nut ice cream and garnished with sprigs of mint.

A good rice pudding needs time to cook, and the best possible ingredients – creamy whole milk and good butter will help to make a wonderful pudding.

baked rice meringue
with bourbon raisins

serves 4–6

225g/8oz muscatel raisins
grated zest of 1 lemon
$\frac{1}{2}$ tsp freshly grated nutmeg
150ml/$\frac{1}{4}$ pt bourbon
110g/4oz pudding rice
50g/2oz granulated sugar
1140ml/2pt milk
50g/2oz butter, plus extra for buttering
   the dish

meringue
3 egg whites
pinch of salt
175g/6oz caster sugar

25g/1oz demerara sugar

Preheat the oven to 180°C/gas mark 4.

Place the raisins in a bowl with the lemon zest, nutmeg and bourbon. Cover, and leave to one side to allow the raisins to absorb the bourbon.

Butter a large pie dish (it needs to be able to hold all the ingredients comfortably) and add the rice and sugar. Pour in the milk, add the butter and stir. Bake on the middle shelf of the oven for 1 hour, stirring occasionally. Add the raisin mixture and stir well into the rice.

Reduce the oven temperature to 150°C/gas mark 2.

To prepare the meringue, whisk the egg whites with a pinch of salt and half the caster sugar until stiff, then gently fold in the remainder of the sugar. Spoon over the top of the rice and bake for a further 20–25 minutes until light golden brown and firm to the touch.

Sprinkle with the demerara sugar and serve hot with yoghurt, or pecan nut ice cream (see page 95).

blueberry
trifle

6 eggs – separated
200g/7oz caster sugar
1 vanilla pod
350g/12oz mascarpone cheese
275ml/1/2pt whipping cream – whipped
350g/12oz blueberries
1 dsp water
juice of 1/2 lemon

1 hot-milk sponge cake
  (see page 115)
150ml/1/4pt sherry

decoration

1 tbsp fresh blueberries
50g/2oz flaked almonds – toasted

Beat the egg yolks and 175g/6oz of the caster sugar in a heatproof bowl until pale and creamy. Add the vanilla pod, slit down one side, and cook over a pan of simmering water for 5–6 minutes, until the mixture thickens slightly and loses its eggy flavour. The best way to test if the mixture is ready is to taste it. Remove from the heat, take out the vanilla pod and allow to cool. When almost cool, add the mascarpone cheese and cream alternately, a little at a time, mixing thoroughly after each addition.

Place the blueberries in a saucepan with the water, remaining sugar and the lemon juice. Heat gently for 1–2 minutes, until the sugar has dissolved, then leave to cool.

Cut the cake into slices about 2.5cm/1in thick and arrange half in the bottom of a large serving dish. Pour over half the sherry, and spoon over half the poached blueberries and half the mascarpone custard. Repeat all the layers, including the sherry, but reserve a little of the blueberry mixture for the top.

Decorate the top layer of mascarpone cream with the remaining poached blueberries, fresh blueberries and almonds. Alternatively serve the trifle in individual bowls or glasses.

Blackberries are in season and at their best from the end of July until the end of September, although you can find them in shops throughout the year. You can also make this sorbet with canned or frozen fruits.

blackberry
sorbet

serves 4–6

275ml/¹/2pt water plus 2–3 dsp
25g/1oz caster sugar
450g/1lb blackberries

110g/4oz granulated sugar
grated zest and juice of 1 lemon
1 egg white – whisked until stiff

Place the 2–3 dsp water and the caster sugar in a saucepan. Heat gently until the sugar has dissolved. Poach the blackberries in this syrup, just to soften them a little. Purée and leave to cool.

Heat the main quantity of water with the granulated sugar and lemon juice. Let the sugar dissolve before bringing the mixture to the boil and bubbling for 2–3 minutes. Allow to cool slightly before adding the lemon zest and juice. Leave until cold. Stir the blackberry purée into the cold syrup. Fold in the whisked egg white and either transfer the mixture to an ice cream machine and follow the instructions, or pour it into a shallow plastic container and place in the coolest part of your freezer for at least 2¹/2–3 hours, whizzing in the food processor several times during freezing to break up the ice crystals. Remove the sorbet from the freezer around 20 minutes before you are ready to serve it.

mango
sorbet

serves 4–6

225g/8oz granulated sugar
275ml/¹/2pt water

2 mangoes – peeled, stoned and cut into chunks

Heat the sugar and water in a saucepan until the sugar has dissolved. Turn up the heat and boil rapidly for 2 minutes. Purée the mango flesh in a blender until smooth, then add to the sugar syrup and mix well. Leave to cool and then chill. Either transfer the mixture to an ice cream machine and follow the instructions, or pour it into a shallow plastic container and place in the coolest part of your freezer for at least 2¹/2–3 hours, whizzing in the food processor several times during freezing to break up the ice crystals. Remove the sorbet from the freezer around 20 minutes before you are ready to serve it.

The flavour of whiskey combines beautifully with tangy lemon in this delicate light pudding.

irish whiskey
syllabub
with toasted pecan nuts

serves 4–6

1 tbsp freshly squeezed lemon juice
grated zest of 1 1/2 lemons
50g/2oz caster sugar
3 tbsp Irish whiskey

275ml/1/2pt double cream – whipped
1 egg white – whisked until stiff
25g/1oz pecan nuts

Mix the lemon juice, two thirds of the lemon zest, the sugar and whiskey in a bowl until the sugar has dissolved. Fold in the cream and then the egg white. Transfer the mixture into tall glasses and chill in the fridge for 1 hour.

Toast the pecan nuts in a dry frying pan until golden, then chop them roughly.

Sprinkle the nuts and remaining lemon zest over the glasses of syllabub and serve.

baking

At the Quincy indoor market – one of the most popular tourist attractions in Boston

Perfect for mopping up all the juices from the New England boiled dinner (see page 56).

(see page 56)

horseradish
soda bread

serves 6

450g/1lb soda bread self-raising flour
1/2 tsp salt
1/2 tsp mustard

1 dsp horseradish sauce
275ml/1/2 pt buttermilk
1 egg – lightly beaten

Preheat the oven to 200°C/gas mark 6.

Sift the flour into a large bowl and add the salt, mustard and horseradish sauce. Add the buttermilk a little at a time and, stirring at first, then using your hand, mix to a soft dough.

Turn out onto a floured surface, knead lightly, then shape either into one large round (cut a deep cross into the top of the large loaf), 4 farls or 4 small round loaves. Place on a baking sheet, brush with egg and bake for 15–20 minutes, until risen, golden and cooked through. The bottom of the loaf should sound hollow when tapped – if not, cook for a further 5 minutes and check again. Alternatively, cook on a preheated large griddle pan for 12–15 minutes.

This is a wonderfully simple bread to make and it smells gorgeous when it's cooking.

bacon, brie and sun-dried tomato
bread

serves 6

275g/10oz plain flour
2 heaped tsp baking powder
1/4 tsp salt
2 eggs – lightly beaten
1/2 tsp English mustard

4 dsp olive oil
175g/6oz rindless maple-cured bacon – diced
110g/4oz Brie – cut into chunks
50g/2oz sun-dried tomatoes – finely sliced
125ml/4floz milk

Preheat the oven to 180°C/gas mark 4. Grease a 450g/1lb loaf tin.

Sieve the flour, baking powder and salt into a bowl. Add the eggs, mustard, olive oil, bacon, two-thirds of the cheese, the sun-dried tomatoes and milk. Mix well to form a soft, sticky dough. Transfer to the prepared tin and press down well. Place the reserved cheese on top of the loaf and bake for around 50 minutes until firm, risen and golden. Turn out onto a cooling rack and serve warm or cold.

You will notice the similarity between these traditional New England biscuits and our scones. This is a great recipe – the biscuits can be made in a food processor in minutes, and are delicious served with jam and cream.

buttermilk
biscuits

makes 8–10

225g/8oz self-raising flour
1/2 tsp baking soda
10g/1/2oz caster sugar
1/2 tsp salt

110g/4oz butter – softened
25g/1oz margarine
125ml/4floz buttermilk

Preheat the oven to 200°C/gas mark 6.

Place the flour, baking soda, sugar, salt, butter, margarine and half of the buttermilk in a food processor. Whizz together and add the remainder of the buttermilk if you need it – the dough just needs to begin to stick together.

Flour a surface and turn the dough out on to it. Knead lightly, then roll out to a thickness of around 1/2in/1cm. Using a round or square cutter cut out 6–8 biscuits. Place on a baking sheet, well spaced out as they will spread during cooking, and bake for 12–15 minutes.

When cooked, wrap in a clean dry tea towel and allow to cool. Serve warm or cold.

The combination of the cranberries with the nuttiness of either walnuts or hazelnuts works a treat in this recipe. The cranberries will burst as the cake cooks, giving a lovely texture and flavour.

new england cranberry
and walnut
teabread

serves 8

110g/4oz caster sugar
2 small eggs
2 dsp sunflower oil
225g/8oz self-raising flour
1/2 tsp baking powder
1/2 tsp bicarbonate of soda

1/2 tsp ground cinnamon
1/4 tsp salt
175g/6oz cranberries
75g/3oz walnuts or hazelnuts –
    coarsely chopped
grated zest of 1 orange

Preheat the oven to 180°C/gas mark 4. Line and grease a 450g/1lb loaf tin.

Whisk the sugar and eggs together until light and fluffy, then gradually add the oil, whisking as you do so. The oil will reduce the volume of the mixture but don't worry about this.

Sift the flour, baking powder, bicarbonate of soda and cinnamon into the mixture and fold in gently, being careful not to overbeat. Add the salt, cranberries, two-thirds of the nuts and half the orange zest. Mix well, then pour the mixture into the prepared tin. Sprinkle with the remainder of the nuts and the orange zest.

Bake for about 45 minutes, until risen, golden and firm to the touch. Turn out and cool on a wire rack. Serve warm or cold – it's delicious buttered.

This cake is lighter than most carrot cakes and is packed with texture and spices.

carrot cake
with maple frosting

serves 8

150ml/¹/4pt sunflower oil
225g/8oz caster sugar
3 egg yolks and 2 egg whites – lightly beaten together
2 carrots (approximately 175g/6oz) – finely grated
50g/2oz dessicated coconut
50g/2oz sultanas
225g/8oz self-raising flour
¹/2 tsp baking powder
¹/2 tsp bicarbonate of soda

¹/2 tsp ground cinnamon
¹/2 tsp ground cloves
¹/2 tsp freshly grated nutmeg
1 egg white – whisked until stiff

frosting
225g/8oz light cream cheese
50g/2oz butter – softened
50g/2oz icing sugar
2 tbsp maple syrup
50g/2oz walnuts or pecan nuts – finely chopped

Preheat the oven to 170°C/gas mark 3. Line and grease a 900g/2lb loaf tin.

Beat the oil with the sugar for 2–3 minutes, then add the beaten egg yolks and whites, grated carrot, coconut and sultanas. Sieve in the flour, baking powder, bicarbonate of soda, cinnamon, cloves and nutmeg and mix well. Using a spatula or metal spoon, gently fold in the stiffly whisked egg white, trying to keep as much air as possible in the mixture.

Pour the mixture into the tin and bake for about 45 minutes, until the cake is risen, browned and firm to the touch. Turn out to cool on a wire rack.

To make the frosting, beat the cream cheese with the butter, icing sugar and maple syrup until smooth. Chill until ready to ice the cake.

Spread the frosting over the top of the cooled cake, and decorate with the nuts.

Squash can be incorporated into cakes in a similar way to carrots, giving a wonderful texture. A great tasting treat for all the family.

nutty squash and
banana loaf

serves 8

110g/4oz butter – softened
110g/4oz soft brown sugar
175g/6oz plain flour
1 1/2 tsp baking powder
1/2 tsp bicarbonate of soda
1/2 tsp ground cinnamon
3 eggs – lightly beaten

1/2 tsp natural vanilla extract
75g/3oz hazelnuts – roughly chopped
50g/2oz ground almonds
2 large ripe bananas – peeled and mashed
110g/4oz prepared pumpkin or squash
  flesh – grated

Preheat the oven to 170°C/gas mark 3. Line and grease a 900g/2lb loaf tin.

In a large bowl, cream the butter with the sugar until light and fluffy.

Sift the flour, baking powder, bicarbonate of soda and cinnamon into another bowl.

Add the eggs and flour alternately to the creamed mixture, a little at a time, ensuring that each addition is well mixed in before adding the next. Fold in the vanilla extract, nuts, bananas and squash. Mix well, then transfer to the prepared tin. Bake for 45–50 minutes, until risen, set and golden. Allow to cool for a few minutes in the tin, then turn out onto a wire rack to cool completely. Serve warm or cold.

This cake does not rise much, but it has a wonderful texture and flavour. It is delicious served warm with yoghurt, or sliced and buttered for afternoon tea.

maple-drizzle
pound cake

serves 8

175g/6oz plain flour
¹/4 tsp salt
¹/4 tsp bicarbonate of soda
grated zest of 2 lemons
75ml/3floz milk
150ml/¹/4pt maple syrup
2 large eggs

110g/4oz caster sugar
75g/3oz butter – softened

for the tin
25g/1oz butter – melted
25g/1oz caster sugar

Preheat the oven to 180°C/gas mark 4. Line a 450g/1lb loaf tin with greaseproof paper, then brush generously with the melted butter and dust with the caster sugar.

Sift the flour, salt and bicarbonate of soda into a large bowl. Add the lemon zest, milk and half the maple syrup, and mix briefly – there should still be flour around the edges of the bowl at this point.

In a separate bowl, whisk the eggs lightly with a fork and stir in the caster sugar until combined. Add this to the flour a little at a time, stirring continuously until smooth, but try not to overbeat. Then stir in the butter.

Transfer the batter to the prepared tin. Bake for 35–45 minutes, until the cake is golden and firm to the touch. Just before the cake is cooked, heat the remaining maple syrup gently in a saucepan.

When the cake is ready, remove it from the tin, peel off the greaseproof paper, and pour over the warmed maple syrup.

This cake is an essential ingredient for blueberry trifle (see page 100), but also delicious on its own, filled with strawberry jam and cream, and dusted with icing sugar.

hot-milk
sponge cake

serves 8

55ml/2floz milk
50g/2oz butter
1/2 tsp natural vanilla extract
5 eggs
110g/4oz caster sugar
125g/4 1/2oz self-raising flour

for the tin
25g/1oz butter – melted
25g/1oz caster sugar

Preheat the oven to 180°C/gas mark 4. Brush a loose-bottomed cake tin measuring 20–23cm/8–9in in diameter generously with the melted butter and dust with the caster sugar.

Place the milk and butter in a saucepan, add the vanilla extract and heat very gently, just until the butter melts. Turn off the heat and set aside.

Beat the eggs with the sugar until light, creamy and doubled in volume. This will take approximately 7–8 minutes. Sift in the flour, a little at a time, mixing as you go. Add the slightly cooled milk and butter mixture, mixing slowly all the time until the milk is completely incorporated. When you add the milk, the volume of the mixture will substantially decrease, but don't worry about this – the cake will rise well in the oven.

Transfer to the prepared tin and bake for approximately 20–25 minutes, until risen, golden and firm to the touch. Turn out onto a wire rack and leave to cool.

The irresistible all-American cookie – perfect with a cup of tea.

fruit and nut
snickerdoodles

makes 16–24

225g/8oz plain flour
1 tsp bicarbonate of soda
1 tsp ground cinnamon
110g/4oz caster sugar
1 egg
1 egg yolk

110g/4oz butter – softened
1 tsp natural vanilla extract
50g/2oz walnuts – finely chopped
110g/4oz currants, raisins or
   dried cranberries

Grease and flour 2 or 3 baking sheets. Sift the flour, bicarbonate of soda and cinnamon into a food processor. Add the sugar, whole egg, egg yolk, butter and vanilla extract. Whizz together until blended. Add the walnuts and currants, raisins or dried cranberries, and whizz again very briefly – for just a few seconds – until everything is combined.

Transfer the mixture to a lightly floured surface and divide it into two, to make it easier to handle. Shape each half into a log shape, then cut each log into 8–12 equal portions. Shape each small piece into a ball and flatten a little on top.

Place the snickerdoodles on the prepared baking sheets, well apart, and transfer to the fridge for around 15 minutes, to firm them up and to prevent them from spreading out during cooking.

Preheat the oven to 180°C/gas mark 4. Bake for 10–12 minutes, until the snickerdoodles are golden and crisp. Cool briefly on the sheets, then transfer to a wire rack and leave until cold. Store in airtight jars.

Chloe and Ellie making fruit
and nut snickerdoodles

These biscuits are always popular with children, and they're very quick and easy to make.

bubble
biscuits

makes 12

150g/5oz butter – softened
75g/3oz soft brown sugar
2 large eggs – lightly beaten
grated zest and juice of $^1/_2$ orange
225g/8oz self-raising flour
$^1/_2$ tsp bicarbonate of soda

50g/2oz rolled oats
50g/2oz granola (see page 14) or muesli
50g/2oz white chocolate chips
50g/2oz raisins, sultanas or dried blueberries

to serve
25g/1oz icing sugar

Preheat the oven to 190°C/gas mark 5. Grease and flour 2 baking sheets.

Cream the butter with the sugar in a large bowl until light and fluffy. Mix in the eggs, and orange zest and juice.

Sift the flour and bicarbonate of soda, a little at a time, into the wet ingredients, mixing lightly between additions. Add the oats, granola, chocolate chips and dried fruit and mix well. If the mixture seems too dry, add a little more egg.

Roll the mixture into rounds about the size of ping pong balls and place, well spaced out, on the prepared baking sheets. Bake for 12–15 minutes and serve warm, dusted with icing sugar.

These are a real treat that can be made in any shape or style.

bramley and bramble
autumn slices

pastry

200g/7oz plain flour

$1/2$ tsp baking powder

110g/4oz butter

25g/1oz ground almonds

50g/2oz caster sugar

$1/4$ tsp natural vanilla extract

1 egg

topping

2 Bramley apples – peeled, cored and sliced

75g/3oz blackberries

4 dsp crab apple jelly or plum jam

$1/2$ tsp cinnamon powder

25g/1oz demerara sugar

to serve

25g/1oz icing sugar

Preheat the oven to 180°C/gas mark 4.

To make the pastry, place the flour, baking powder, butter, almonds, sugar, vanilla extract and egg in a food processor. Whizz until the ingredients come together. Turn out onto a lightly floured surface and roll out to line a square tin, measuring approximately 23cm/9in square. Press down well into the tin.

In a bowl, mix together the apples, blackberries, jelly or jam, and cinnamon. Spread this mixture over the pastry base, and sprinkle the demerara sugar on the top. Bake in the oven for 30–35 minutes.

When ready, allow to cool briefly before turning out and cutting into squares. Dust with icing sugar and serve.

old-fashioned
gingerbread
with walnuts and raisins

110g/4oz butter
110g/4oz soft brown sugar
1 dsp honey or syrup
1 dsp treacle
175g/6oz self-raising flour
50g/2oz wholemeal flour

2 tsp ground ginger
1 tsp mixed spice
50g/2oz walnuts – finely chopped
50g/2oz raisins
1 egg – lightly beaten
150ml/1/4pt milk

Preheat the oven to 170°C/gas mark 3. Grease a 450g/1lb loaf tin.

Melt the butter in a saucepan over a low heat. Add the sugar, honey and treacle and stir until the sugar has dissolved. Set aside for a moment to cool a little.

Sift the self-raising flour and wholemeal flour into a bowl. Add the ginger, mixed spice, two-thirds of the walnuts and the raisins.

Pour the slightly cooled butter mixture into the flour, add the egg and milk and mix well. Pour into the prepared tin, sprinkle with the remaining walnuts, and bake for 25–30 minutes, until firm to the touch.

This is a really lovely celebratory cake – perfect for Christmas entertaining.

cranberry and apple
upside-down cake

serves 8

topping

25g/1oz butter

50g/2oz caster sugar

3 cooking apples – peeled and cut into wedges

75g/3oz cranberries

50g/2oz nuts (hazel, pecan or brazil all work very well)

cake

150g/5oz butter – softened

150g/5oz caster sugar

3 small eggs – lightly beaten

175g/6oz self-raising flour – sieved

50g/2oz ground almonds

zest of 1 lemon

1/4 tsp vanilla essence

Preheat the oven to 190°C/gas mark 5.

Make the caramel by heating together the butter and sugar in a saucepan until almost toffee-like. Pour into the base of a solid-bottomed non-stick, round cake tin, around 18–20cm/7–8in in diameter. Carefully place the apple wedges on top of the toffee and scatter over the cranberries and nuts. If you prefer, you can make a pattern with the apples, cranberries and nuts – this will be the top of the cake when you turn it out.

In a bowl cream together the butter and sugar until light and fluffy. Stirring all the time, add the eggs and flour alternately. Stir in the almonds, lemon zest and vanilla essence. If the mixture seems too heavy, add a little milk. Spoon this mixture over the fruit, smooth and bake for 30–35 minutes until risen, golden and firm to the touch.

Allow to cool for 5 minutes before turning out onto a flat plate, with the cranberries, apples and nuts on the top. Serve warm or cold with cream or yoghurt.

glossary of ingredients and techniques

ancho chillies

Ancho chillies are dried poblano chillies. They are large and mild, with a sweetish, rich flavour. If you can't find ancho chillies, try a mild, fresh red chilli instead, deseeded, and grilled until blackened and soft. Peel off the skin and it's ready to use!

blind baking

Blind baking ensures crisp pastry that shouldn't leak. To blind bake, line the pie dish or tin with the pastry. Prick it several times on the bottom with a fork, and then line the pastry shell with greaseproof paper. Fill with dried peas, beans or lentils to prevent the pastry from rising. Then follow the instructions in the recipe regarding time and temperature.

chillies

Fresh chillies are a delicious, spicy addition to many dishes. Go for chillies that are firm and smooth skinned. It's hard to tell how hot each chilli will be before you try it, but, in general, smaller chillies are hotter than large ones. The heat in chillies comes from their seeds and the white membrane surrounding them, so remove these before using the chillies. Always wash your hands thoroughly after handling chillies, or wear rubber gloves, as the active ingredient in them can burn your eyes and skin.

cockles and mussels

Always buy fresh cockles and mussels, and discard any that have open or broken shells. Scrub them well, removing any beards, and rinse them thoroughly in several changes of fresh cold water. To cook, place them in a heavy-bottomed pan with water and simmer for around 5 minutes, until their shells have opened. Discard any that do not open during cooking.

cranberries

The cranberry is one of the few fruits that is native to North America, and it is widely believed that pilgrims served cranberries at the first Thanksgiving meal in the seventeenth century. Cranberry sauce is one of the staples of Thanksgiving and Christmas dinner, although this bouncing berry is enormously versatile and delicious in many dishes. Cranberries are in season in late autumn but are now available for much of the year. If you can't find fresh, frozen or dried cranberries (craisins) are a good alternative.

maple syrup

Producers make maple syrup by boiling the sap of maple trees – it takes forty gallons of sap to produce just one gallon of syrup. It's now widely available, but make sure that you are buying the pure product (100 per cent maple syrup) rather than an artificially flavoured imitation. Traditionally served with pancakes and waffles for breakfast, it's a versatile ingredient that you can use in many different dishes, as you'll see in these recipes! It's delicious as a sweetener in coffee, or poured over vanilla ice cream.

pumpkins and squashes

Choose pumpkins and squashes that are firm and heavy for their size. You will need to deseed and peel them before using – although you can roast wedges of pumpkin and squash with their skin on, and scoop out the flesh when it is soft. If you can't track down fresh pumpkin or squash, canned pumpkin can be a useful alternative in recipes that call for pumpkin purée.

sterilising jars

Sterilising jars is an important part of the jam-making process as it ensures that there are no traces of dirt in the jars that might cause the jam to spoil. Wash the jars thoroughly in warm soapy water, rinse well and then place them in an oven, preheated to 190°C/gas mark 5, for 15–20 minutes. It's best to pour hot jam into warm jars to reduce the risk of them cracking.

Acknowledgements

A very big thank you to everyone who helped in the making of *Jenny Bristow USA*. I have managed to surround myself with the very best people who shower me with inspiration, encouragement and, most of all, laughter along the way.

Thanks to all the team at UTV under the direction and guidance of Bernie Morrison, a true free spirit, whose support and friendship is unwavering. The entire team of Mary, Billy, Sam, Ivan, PJ, Maureen, Nan, Vera and Rosario who I work with. You all know who you are and how special you are in all that we do.

A special thank you to the publishing team at Blackstaff Press who do such a great job and with such ease, or maybe it just seems that way. Thank you to Patsy Horton and Helen Wright, my new editor, who has managed to manoeuvre me along the path of writing this book ever so gently.

Thank you to Robert McKeag, photographer and lifelong friend. Thank you also to Jeff Scher who was the photographer for the US location shots, to Julie McMaster, food stylist, and to Wendy Dunbar who designed the book.

Thank you to everyone at the Ulster-American Folk Park (www.folkpark.com) for all your help.

Many thanks also to Helen Turkington at the Fabric Library, Cookstown and Newbridge, County Kildare; to Paddy McNeill of Beeswax, Kilrea, for sourcing the freestanding dressers and cupboards; to Sally at Floral Designs, Ballymena; Lakeland Limited; Star Glass Ltd in Hastings; Poole Pottery in Dorset; Dunoon Ceramics Ltd, Staffordshire; Richardson Sheffield Housewares; Tableware at Pimpernel; to Hilary and Ian Robinson at Presence, Newtownards for so much hard work in coordinating china, pottery and dishes for the programmes; to Belleek Pottery for coordinating china for the Thanksgiving programme; Martha's House in Wellington Street, Ballymena, and Queen Street, Coleraine, for the redecoration of the barn studio, curtains, fabrics, dishes and decorations; to all the amazing people we met while travelling and filming in New England, and to all who contributed to the programmes and helped make it such an enjoyable experience.

Thank you all so much.

Index

First published in 2007 by
Blackstaff Press,
4c Heron Wharf, Sydenham Business Park,
Belfast BT3 9LE,
in association with UTV

ISBN 978-0-85640-789-5

www.blackstaffpress.com
www.jennybristow.com